Homestyle

SOUTHEAST ASIAN

Cooking

BY

RANI KING & CHANDRA KHAN

THE CROSSING PRESS
FREEDOM, CALIFORNIA

For Mum and Dad, for
believing in us

Copyright © 1998 by Rani King & Chandra Khan
Cover design by Victoria May
Photographs by Steve Baxter, Food prepared by Oona Van Der Berg, Styling by Marian Price
Step-by-step interior illustrations by Rodney Paull
Printed in the U.S.A.

First published in England in 1996 by Judy Piatkus (Publishers) Ltd.

For information on bulk purchases or group discounts for this and other Crossing Press titles, please contact our Special Sales Manager at 800-777-1048 x214.

Visit our Web site on the Internet: www.crossingpress.com

Library of Congress Cataloging-in-Publication Data

King, Rani.
    Homestyle Southeast Asian cooking / by Rani King & Chandra Khan.
        p. cm. — (Homestyle cooking series)
    Previously published as: Tigerlily: flavours of the Orient.
    Includes index.
    ISBN 0-89594-905-9 (pbk.)
    1. Cookery, Southeast Asian. I. Khan, C. (Chandra C.), 1952–.
II. Title. III. Series.
TX724.5S68K56   1998
641.5959–dc21   98-10583
                                                       CIP

CONTENTS

ACKNOWLEDGMENTS

We would like to thank Mum and Dad for believing "their little girls could achieve anything"; John for ruining two cars and his back lugging Tiger Lily products around for seven years; Howard for his support and encouragement; Justin, the greatest fan of our products; Neisha for being there with us right from the start; and Johnny and Julian for being patient guinea pigs for our recipes.

Chandra's thanks go to all whose professional advice helped make Tiger Lily a success: Ron Gardiner of NLTEC, Albert Wright of BEC, and all at NatWest. Not forgetting BT Plc for being a good employer for 17 years, then releasing her to carve a new career.

Rani's thanks go to Elaine Norman and Chris Turner. Tony Shillingford, Usha Sharma, Mike Boland, Gillian Dyer, and Tom Adams for their encouragement when things were difficult, and to the Department for Education and Employment who allowed her to develop her journalistic talents to the full.

Finally, our grateful thanks to Helen Hague, whose news article boosted our efforts on to a waiting world, and our customers for their faithful patronage.

To all those mentioned above, and to those we have not been able to name through lack of space, goes our love!

INTRODUCTION

This book introduces recipes from China, Malaysia, Thailand, Indonesia, and Sri Lanka which can be easily followed and cooked with the minimum of time and fuss. Or, to paraphrase Shirley Conran who freed so many of us from the tyranny of the kitchen in the seventies with the battle cry "Life is too short to stuff a mushroom," we say "Life is too short to grate a coconut!"

Like many women today, our lives are a careful balancing act between family, work, and socializing. Although we love good food, we simply do not have the time to spend hours in the kitchen laboriously producing gourmet meals. All our recipes have therefore been designed to produce authentic tastes without the fuss and mystique that so often surround Asian cooking.

We hope you will enjoy trying out our recipes and that your friends and family will enjoy the results. But most of all, we hope you will have as much fun reading this book as we have had writing it, and reminiscing about how it all started…

When asked where she was going, my sister Chandra, aged just two, apparently tucked me (two weeks) under her arm firmly and said, continuing towards the lake outside the house, "I'm going to drown the cat because it wails so much."

This could well have been the shortest working relationship in history. However, I was saved that day and lived to repay her attentions. By the time I was two myself (and Chandra just four), we had managed to inject each other with my grandfather's insulin, take his deadly heart pills and have our stomachs pumped out, and I had (literally) given Chandra a close shave with our father's cutthroat razor. She bears the scars on her chin to this day.

Not for nothing were the servants terrified of the "terrible twins." However, we were always close and, as we grew, we shared an increasing love of food. Chandra's first words in Thai were "*king kao!*" (eat rice), and if set down, she would immediately toddle towards the kitchen. Her legs grew so fat and her thighs forced so wide apart that her feet turned in and she was forced to wear corrective shoes. Much of our interest in food derived from our parents' mistaken belief that fat children were healthy children. Mother paid each of our amahs or nannies (there were four of them, one for each of her daughters) a bonus if we put on weight at the weekly weigh-in. It was a bit like Weight Watchers in reverse.

This resulted in them running behind us with bowls of rice balls which they would try and force-feed us, like baby birds, at every opportunity. We would shin along the almost horizontal coconut tree trunks (we lived on the beach in Sri Lanka and the fierce sea winds molded all the trees landwards), and when our amahs almost managed to get to us, we would bounce up and down vigorously until they fell off.

We had an idyllic childhood traveling around the world in the wake of our very glamorous parents, a Sri Lankan diplomat and Chinese film-star mother. In our early days we were cared for by a retinue of servants from whom we learned many tricks of the catering trade. Dad's posting to the Court of St. James in London, and to our exciting Embassy in Washington, D.C., gave us access to food cooked by the best diplomatic chefs in the world. We became used to eating smoked salmon, caviar, and lobster and dining out in the best restaurants. Now we realize how very fortunate we were, but then we took it much for granted. However, our palates benefited from this early exposure to gourmet food, and the combinations of unusual ingredients, prepared with imagination and panache, have influenced our own recipes.

Although we moved in very grand circles on the embassy circuit, back home we lived idyllically simple lives very close to nature. We spent wonderful days and nights eating with the fisher folk who lived in thatched palm huts on the beach outside our grand gates. We both well remember the most wonderful rice and curries that came from earthen *chatties* or round pots cooked over open fires. We also remember the way the men would come home in the early hours of the morning, phosphorous flying like showers of stars from the bows of their catamarans. And recall the thrill of seeing the myriad colored fish that we now see in aquariums, but then would be bundled unceremoniously into the nearest cooking utensil.

Our love of good food and handed-down family recipes from around the world inspired us to form our company, Tiger Lily—Oriental Fire! Specializing in the authentic tastes of Sri Lanka and the Pacific Rim (i.e., Thailand, Malaysia, Singapore, and Indonesia). We launched a range of instant Oriental spice mixes, relishes, and other culinary essentials, all with a shelf life of at least a year, but with no additives, preservatives, or colorants.

Now we open our well-thumbed, hand-written recipe books and share with you the food we prepare lovingly for our friends and families. Nothing would give us greater pleasure than to see a copy of our book in your kitchen, stained, dog-eared (to mark your favorite recipe) and even scribbled in. This would show us that you are adapting the recipes to suit *yourself* and your families.

We love food, we respect food. It is our way of expressing love for our nearest and dearest, but we do not let it rule our lives. Exotic meals can be made with the minimum of effort and, to be honest, a little inventive tweaking.

Using the basics found in most people's cupboards, with a few additions, you too can replicate the fiery taste of the Orient!

Ingredients vary in strength. For example, the smaller the chile, the hotter the taste. Ground red pepper also varies in its potency. Likewise fish sauce and even soy sauce can have quite different strengths. We have tried to keep the recipes in this book as standard as possible, and you should adjust the ingredients according to your own taste.

We have included notes on spices and sauces that may be unfamiliar to Western readers, but if some ingredients are not available to you, don't hesitate to substitute according to your imagination and experience. The result may not be "authentic," but it will be well-cooked, interesting, and delicious.

Incidentally, we debated whether to give authentic names for all these recipes but decided against it for two reasons. Firstly, because as we have added our own twist to several classical southeast Asian recipes, it would not be fair to claim that they are the original versions. And secondly, do you really want to know that Fried Rice Sticks is called *Phat Wun Sen* in Thailand? We promised you no mystique and no frills and so we have described most dishes by their contents to help you decide whether you will enjoy them or not.

Bon Appétit!

PLANNING A MEAL

Serving Asian meals is simplicity itself. Unlike the Western jack-in-the-box ritual, where the frazzled host or hostess is up and down all night serving three or more courses in turn, each one often requiring individual heating up, our meals are mostly placed on the table together except for the desserts. Very few of these are served hot so they can be prepared well in advance. More often, we would end the meal with a selection of refreshing tropical fruit cut into beautiful shapes.

We frequently cook the food a few days in advance (believing that curries taste better as they mature and the flavors have a chance to develop) and then heat the dishes together, in the oven or microwave, before serving. Remember to cover the dishes so the food does not dry out.

Everyone helps themselves to a little of everything, including soup. Some homes invest in a lazy Susan, a round serving area in the middle of the dining table which swivels around. Dishes can then be offered around the table without anyone having to move.

We prefer to eat most curry dishes lukewarm. This is very convenient, as food can be heated, dished out, and left on the table to cool before your guests arrive. Sometimes the spicy heat of a curry coupled with a too-high serving temperature can be overwhelming and ruin the taste of a carefully prepared dish.

We like lots of different side dishes, plenty of vegetables and not very much meat or other protein. Our family meals include one protein dish, one vegetable dish, and a rice, noodle, or flour-based accompaniment.

Although stir-frying takes only minutes, stir-fried food should be served as soon as possible after cooking. We have prepared stir-fried dishes in advance and then heated them, but they are not at their best. The preparation for Chinese food is quite lengthy, especially washing and cutting the ingredients. For entertaining, our tip is to prepare everything the night before, including measuring out the ingredients on to a single tray or place, then cover with plastic wrap until the next day.

DRINKS

We are often asked what type of beverages go well with our meals. There are some very good Asian beers, but normally a refreshing fruit-based drink is offered. Freshly squeezed lime juice, sweetened with sugar, and served in a tall glass with plenty of ice cubes, is a favorite. So is passionfruit juice, or mangoes or watermelons whirled in a blender, and served icy cold. In Sri Lanka, a favorite drink is iced tea or coffee. Both are flavored with vanilla or cardamom pods and sweetened with condensed milk. Chinese meals are best served with clear weak tea—flavored with jasmine or orange flowers, lychee, passionfruit, or mango. A pot of tea is placed on the table and frequently replenished with hot water.

One special recipe enjoyed in Sri Lanka, Indonesia, and Malaysia is *Falooda*—a milk-based, rose-water-flavored drink with pieces of seaweed (*agar agar*) jelly, strands of cellophane noodles, and *kasa-kasa*. This is a type of small seed (*tulsi* in Indian) which expands in water to form a jelly ball surrounding a small crunchy middle. In Sri Lanka, *kasa-kasa* is believed to lower body heat and is added to orange juice or barley water. In India, drinking *lassi* is a good way to quench fiery hot curries. Whisk equal amounts of yogurt and water together and either flavor with a little salt or, more acceptably, sugar and vanilla, rose or orange water, or a pinch of ground cardamom, and serve with crushed ice.

MENUS

We have given some menu suggestions below. Sometimes it is better to serve one or two of the dishes first, as starters. We have indicated these with an asterisk (*).

Menu 1: Sri Lankan

Mulligatawny or Lentil Soup
Sri Lankan Hoppers (and Egg Hoppers)
and/or Coconut Rotis and Hodi
Coconut Sambol
Mallung
Sri Lankan Lamb & Spinach Curry
Vattalapan

This menu has several interesting flavors, many of which will be new to readers. The *hodi* (Coconut Soup) is poured on the *roti* only enough to moisten it. The sambols and Vegetable Mallung really spice up the meal. Vattalapan is a delicious cardamom-flavored custard served ice-cold.

Menu 2: Sri Lankan

*Onion Bhajiis
*Mint & Yogurt Dip
Rasam
Biriyani
Salt Fish Curry and/or Beef Smoore
Pineapple Curry
Tomato, Cucumber, & Onion Sambol
Fresh green leaf salad
Avocado Ice Cream

Here the spicy Onion Bhajiis and Mint and Yogurt Dip starter give a taste of what is to come. The heat of the Biriyani, curries, and Beef Smoore is balanced by the freshness of the Tomato, Cucumber, & Onion Sambol. Sip the *Rasam* throughout the meal.

Avocado Ice Cream is a beautiful green dessert, very rich and sumptuous, but a lovely way to end a quite savory meal.

Menu 3: Chinese

Hot Sour Soup or Egg Drop Soup
Chicken Rice
Cucumber Batons
Cheena Patas Prawns and/or Beef Rendang
Stir-Fried Beans and/or Quick Fried Bean Sprouts
Sambol Ulek
Steamed Butter Cake with Ginger Cream

Hot Sour Soup is well named, but if you want a tamer start to your meal, try Egg Drop Soup instead. Chicken Rice is a meal in itself. Married with fiery Cheena Patas Prawns and vegetables and delicious dry Beef Rendang curry, followed by Butter Cake with Ginger Cream, this meal is easily prepared but tastes out of this world.

Menu 4: Malaysian

Fried "Seaweed"
Wontons
Satay and Sauce and/or Jewel Fish
Compressed Rice Cakes
Rasam
Turtle "Eggs"

Starting with "Fried Seaweed" and finishing with a dessert called "Turtle Eggs," this menu has a definite ocean theme! The *Rasam* adds an unexpected sharp note, which cuts through the richness of the fried dishes. Sip it throughout the meal to refresh the palate. This meal looks so lovely—with the deep green of the Seaweed, the browns and reds of the satay and sauce or the ravishing colors of Jewel Fish, then the pure white of the rice cakes. Textures are a key to this meal, too: crispy and crunchy, then smooth and creamy.

Menu 5: Thai

Tom Yum Kung
*Paper-Wrapped Chicken and Snowpeas
*Quick Plum Sauce
Nam Prik
Char Sui Pork
Peking Pancakes
Cucumber Batons and Shredded spring onion
Lo Mein (Noodles with Beef and Vegetables)
Tiger Lily Tamarind Fish (optional)
Almond Tea

What a sensational menu! Starting with Thailand's favorite soup and intriguing Paper-wrapped Chicken served with a sweet sauce, the happy eaters progress through dainty pancakes which they stuff at the table with cucumber and shredded scallions, then cautiously dip in fiery *Nam Prik* (hot shrimp sauce) and Plum Sauce. Then come noodles and, perhaps, unusual spicy Tamarind Fish. The meal ends with icy clear sweetened water with creamy diamonds of almond-flavored gelatin. Great fun to eat and easy to cook—everything can be prepared in advance and finished off a few minutes before serving.

Menu 6: Party Buffet

Chicken Batons
Selection of dips and Gado Gado
Mixed Pakoras
Quick and Easy Naan Bread (make mini ones)
Shrimp Toasts
Bombay Mix
Tiger Lily Sweet & Sour Pork Ribs
Sweet and Sour Eggs
Marshmallows
Steamed Butter Cake

This menu will keep vegetarians and meat-eaters equally happy. Cut each Sweet and Sour Egg into 4 segments, the Shrimp Toasts into triangles and the ribs into bite-sized pieces. We enjoy color and texture in our food and this menu laid out on a crisp white tablecloth looks fabulous.

For 25 people, use recipe quantities for 6 to 8, and make 4 times the recipe for the cake.

For 50 people, use recipe quantities for 12 to 16, and make 8 cakes.

INGREDIENTS & ESSENTIAL RECIPES

There are a few essentials you will need before you start using this book.

The essential tools are a mortar and pestle or electric coffee grinder, a blender, some sharp knives, and a wok or deep-fryer.

In the East, our trusty mortar and pestle (usually made of stone) acts as a grinder and blender. We use it to pulverize ingredients such as whole spices, ginger, chiles, and garlic. In the West, with the variety of machines available, we suggest that whole spices are ground in a coffee grinder, sauces and liquids are achieved with a blender, food processors are used for fine chopping and making pastes, while garlic can be crushed with a traditional garlic crusher. If a recipe requires minced ginger, an ordinary cheese grater does the job extremely well.

If you can afford it (and they are now very reasonably priced), we strongly advise you to invest in an electric rice cooker. The sheer bliss of automatic rice cooking will free you to experiment and banish forever grainy uncooked kernels or gummy disasters.

Essential Ingredients

Ginger

Garlic

Soy sauce (we tend to use the darker variety as it is stronger)

Sugar (dark brown or white)

Salt

Vinegar (we always use rice wine)

Vegetable oil (any vegetable oil or peanut or sunflower but *not* olive oil) and sesame oil

Black or white pepper

Sherry (sweet or dry but we usually use sweet)

Fresh chiles (remove the seeds for less heat—we prefer to leave them in)

Ground red pepper, coriander, cumin, and turmeric

Cinnamon sticks

Cloves

Coconut milk (canned)

Onions

Heinz tomato ketchup

Crunchy peanut butter

Cornstarch

Chicken stock cubes (Knorr is best)

Ground mixed spice

Optional Ingredients

Dried prawns
Ginger wine
Galangal
Lemongrass
Curry leaves
Pandanus leaf (*rampe*)
Kaffir lime leaves
Straw oyster mushrooms
Dried tamarind (in a block)
Shrimp paste (*blachan*)
Fish sauce
Jaggery (palm sugar)
Maldive fish
Dried wood ear Chinese mushrooms
Whole cardamom pods
Tung chi (preserved Chinese vegetables)

When we give food workshops, we ask the audience to name some of the essential ingredients needed for Continental cooking—say Italian. Most will be able to reel off some or all of the following: garlic, onions, carrots, tomatoes, oregano, thyme, olive oil, bay leaves, parsley, basil, and lemon juice.

However, when we ask them to say what they need to cook Asian meals they are rather vague. We will let you in on a secret—if you can memorize some of the following list, you will soon be turning out restaurant-quality meals at home. Start with garlic, ginger, coriander (the whole plant—leaves, stalk, root, and seeds ground to a powder), ground cumin and turmeric, lemon or lime juice and rind, lemongrass, galangal, oil (vegetable, peanut or corn and sesame), onions, scallions, soy sauce, brown sugar, cornstarch, fish sauce, coconut milk, and, of course, chiles (whole and fresh, dried whole, crushed or in powder form). Those wishing for more authenticity should track down maldive fish, dried shrimp or prawns, *blachan* (shrimp

paste), curry leaves, *rampe* (pandanus), and kaffir lime leaves.

Generally the preparation is as follows: crush the garlic and ginger (or galangal), fry in hot oil, add the onions, then the meat, fish, chicken, or vegetables, a selection of seasonings and some liquid. Simmer until the ingredients are cooked. If stir-frying, the minimum of liquid is added and the cooking is done over a fierce heat. These standard methods cover most recipes. The only finishing for some dishes is the addition of coconut milk and lime or lemon juice. We always recommend that you serve little dishes of chile sauce, *Balichaw* or Vietnamese Dipping Sauce for those who like their food extra spicy.

We usually serve all the savory dishes (including soups) at once on or in communal dishes. Guests help themselves to what they want and eat the dishes in whatever order they like. It is not against the rules to sip the soup inbetween mouthfuls of rice, curry, etc. Desserts are mostly a selection of the luscious fruits that grow so prolifically in our countries. When offering any of the cooked desserts, we find it best to do so in small amounts, as they are often very rich.

ESSENTIAL RECIPES

The quick and easy way to really good Asian foods is to make your own curry powders, pastes, and sauces. Set aside a weekend to make a batch and keep the pastes and sauces in the refrigerator. Not only will you save the money you would have spent buying inferior products at inflated prices, but you will have the satisfaction of making your own. Start with the Roasted Sri Lankan Curry Powder. The flavor is quite unique.

Roasted Sri Lankan Curry Powder

MAKES ABOUT 1 POUND (3 CUPS)

This is a dark, intensely fragrant powder that is hot but also aromatic, and totally different from Indian curry powders. Sri Lanka (meaning "resplendent island") has many names: Taprobane; Serendipity—the happy knack of finding something good while searching for something else (supposedly coined by Marco Polo when he stumbled across Sri Lanka while looking for India); Ceylon; and the Spice Island. It gained this last name because nearly every known spice is grown there and it was once a center of the spice trade.

Sri Lankan housewives have access to homegrown curry leaves, *rampe* (pandanus), lemongrass, and pepper, and those fortunate enough to own land have clove and cinnamon trees and most of the other spices, too. In the past, homegrown and ground curry powders were the mark of the proud homemaker, although now modern mills produce very good mixes. We think it is still worth taking the initial trouble to make your own.

INGREDIENTS

5 oz dried red chiles (about 1 cup)	1 teaspoon cloves
1 1/3 cups coriander seeds	1 teaspoon cardamom pods
10 tablespoons cumin seeds	2 tablespoons black peppercorns
10 tablespoons fennel seeds	2 teaspoons mustard seeds
1 teaspoon fenugreek seeds	5 inches *rampe* or pandanus, chopped (optional)
2 sticks of cinnamon, each about 2 inches long	2 tablespoons ground rice

METHOD

■ Preheat the oven to 400° F. Spread the chiles and spices in a single layer on a baking sheet and roast for about 10 minutes.

■ Cool, then grind the whole spices in a blender or coffee grinder until smooth.

■ In a heavy-bottomed frying pan, dry-roast the ground rice until it starts turning a light golden brown.

■ Add the roasted spices and *rampe* and roast until the mixture becomes quite a dark brown. Keep stirring so as not to burn the spices.

■ When cool, store in an airtight container.

Garam Masala

This spice mix is sprinkled over cooked curries or added at the end of the cooking time. Use either ounces or tablespoons to measure the ingredients. Like all spices, garam masala should not be made or stored in large quantities. Fresh is best.

INGREDIENTS

1 part coriander seeds	4 parts cardamom pods or 4 parts cardamom seeds
1 part black peppercorns	
2 parts cumin seeds	1 part cinnamon sticks, broken into small pieces
2 parts cloves	

METHOD

■ Preheat the oven to 400° F and roast the spices for 10 minutes.

■ Cool, then place in a blender or coffee grinder and reduce to a fine powder. Do not use a food processor or it may damage the machine.

■ Sift the powder and store in an airtight container.

ABOUT THAI CURRY PASTES

Thai cuisine relies on a combination of several flavors—spicy hot, sour, fishy (using strong dried prawn paste or lighter fish sauce), either clear or milky (using coconut milk), and often sweet. The essential ingredients are galangal (a type of aromatic ginger root) and lemongrass.

We have given recipes for a selection of pastes that can be made up and stored in the refrigerator. They are very hot, so only use between 2 teaspoons and 2 tablespoons of each in 1 pound ingredients—enough for a meal for 4 to 6 people.

Tastes vary, so some of you will be diving in at the deep end and ladling it in. The potency of chiles also varies. Those not used to the searingly hot tastes of Sri Lanka and Thailand are advised to treat these recipes with caution and try 1 teaspoon at a time. All these pastes will last for at least a week in the refrigerator. Store in airtight containers.

Once you know how much you will use for each meal, you can do what we do and freeze individual portions in small plastic bags.

Each recipe should make enough paste for 2 to 4 meals for 4 people.

Thai Red Curry Paste 1

SERVES 2 TO 4

This curry paste is very hot and spicy. It is good in Thai soups and curries that are clear and do not use coconut milk.

INGREDIENTS

3/4 cup chopped fresh red chiles	1 teaspoon chopped coriander root
1/3 cup chopped garlic	1 tablespoon *blachan* (shrimp paste) or 2 tablespoons dried shrimp
3 tablespoons chopped lemongrass	
1 teaspoon chopped galangal or ginger	2 tablespoons oil

METHOD

- Grind all the ingredients together, using a mortar and pestle or a blender.

- Store in the refrigerator in an airtight container.

Thai Red Curry Paste 2

SERVES 2 TO 4

This paste is more aromatic, and the addition of coconut makes it somewhat milder and creamier.

INGREDIENTS

25 fresh red chiles, chopped	1 teaspoon grated lime rind
4 scallions or 1 large onion, chopped	1/2 teaspoon ground coriander
2 tablespoons vegetable oil	3 stalks lemongrass, crushed
1 tablespoon chopped galangal or ginger	1/2 teaspoon caraway seeds
2 tablespoons fish sauce	2 tablespoons coconut milk

METHOD

- Combine all the ingredients and process to a smooth paste in a food processor.

- Store in an airtight bottle and refrigerate. It will last for at least a week.

Thai Green Curry Paste 1

SERVES 2 TO 4

The green of this curry paste comes from the fresh coriander (cilantro) leaves. Although this paste will last for up to a week in the refrigerator, it should be used within 2 days for maximum impact, color, and flavor.

INGREDIENTS

15 green chiles, chopped	1 teaspoon *blachan* (shrimp paste) or 2 teaspoons dried shrimp
4 spring scallions or 1 large onion, chopped	3 stalks lemongrass, crushed
3 garlic cloves, roughly chopped	1 teaspoon ground coriander
2 tablespoons oil	4 tablespoons or 1 bunch fresh coriander (cilantro) leaves, chopped
1 tablespoon chopped galangal or ginger	Juice and grated rind of 2 limes
2 tablespoons fish sauce	3 fresh kaffir lime leaves (optional)
1 tablespoon sugar	

METHOD

■ Combine all the ingredients and process to a smooth paste in a food processor.

Thai Green Curry Paste 2

SERVES 2 TO 4

This paste is creamier and more aromatic. Use in curries that include coconut milk.

INGREDIENTS

3/4 cup chopped green chiles	1 tablespoon ground coriander
1 tablespoon black peppercorns, ground	1 tablespoon ground turmeric
4 scallions or 1 large onion, chopped	1 tablespoon ground cumin
2 tablespoons chopped garlic	3 stalks lemongrass, crushed
4 tablespoons chopped fresh coriander (cilantro) (including the root)	1 tablespoon *blachan* (shrimp paste) or 2 tablespoons dried shrimp
1 tablespoon grated lemon rind	3 tablespoons oil
2 tablespoons salt	1 cup grated coconut

METHOD

■ Combine all the ingredients and process to a smooth paste in a food processor.

Sri Lankan Curry Sauce

**SERVES ABOUT
1 CUP SAUCE
OR
16 PORTIONS**

This sauce is used in several recipes in the book, such as Sri Lankan Lamb and Spinach Curry (page 102). To use it in your own curry recipes, simply brown the meat, fish, or other main ingredients of your choice, then add the curry sauce, bring to a boil, then lower the heat and simmer for about 15 minutes until the curry thickens, stirring constantly.

INGREDIENTS

4 garlic cloves, roughly chopped	2 teaspoons dried maldive fish or dried shrimp, grated or powdered (optional)
5 inch piece ginger, peeled and roughly chopped	1 tablespoon Roasted Sri Lankan Curry Powder (p. 17)
2 medium onions, roughly chopped	3 teaspoons ground turmeric
1 2/3 cups water	4 teaspoons salt
2 (15-ounce) cans tomatoes	6 curry leaves (optional)
2 tablespoons oil (preferably coconut oil)	1 cup coconut milk

METHOD

■ Put the garlic, ginger, onions, and a little of the water in a blender or food processor and process until creamy. Set aside.

■ Purée the tomatoes in the same blender. Set aside.

■ Heat the oil in a pan and add the garlic mixture. Keep stirring until all the water evaporates and the mixture begins to brown.

■ Add the maldive fish or dried shrimp, curry powder, turmeric, salt, and curry leaves, if using. Stir until the mixture begins to form a paste and the oil begins to separate.

■ Add the coconut milk, tomatoes, and the rest of the water, covering the pan to prevent spitting. Bring to a boil, then simmer for 15 to 20 minutes. Canned tomatoes vary in the amount of liquid they contain. Your sauce should be thick and fragrant. Taste and add extra salt if necessary.

■ Freeze in 4 separate bags or containers or in ice cube trays for easy-to-use individual blocks.

Balichaw

DRY SHRIMP APPETIZER

SERVES 4 TO 6

This popular Burmese sambol will keep for up to a month in the refrigerator, stored in a clean, dry, glass jar with an airtight screw-on lid. An excellent standby to pep up curries and stir-fries alike, *Balichaw* is also delicious sprinkled onto soup. Try adding a small teaspoonful to omelets, or in a baked potato.

INGREDIENTS

2 to 3 tablespoons vegetable oil	1/2 teaspoon *blachan* (shrimp paste)
1 medium onion, thinly sliced	2 tablespoons rice wine vinegar
5 garlic cloves, thinly sliced	1 teaspoon salt
2 ounces dried shrimp	1 teaspoon ground red pepper

METHOD

■ Heat 2 tablespoons oil in a frying pan and add the onion and garlic. Fry over a high heat until golden brown and crispy, stirring all the time. Add extra oil if necessary.

■ Remove the onion and garlic from the oil with a slotted spoon and dry on paper towels.

■ Add the shrimp to the oil in the frying pan and fry for at least 3 minutes, stirring all the time until they become crispy.

■ Mash the shrimp paste with the vinegar, salt, and red pepper and add to the pan.

■ Stir the contents of the pan over a medium heat until the mixture becomes dry. Remove from the heat, and add the onion and garlic.

■ Cool, then store in the refrigerator for up to a month.

Nam Prik

HOT SHRIMP SAUCE

SERVES 4

Dynamite! This hot mix is much loved by Thais who use it as a dipping sauce with fresh-cut raw vegetables and small batons of fried fish, cold meat and chicken. It's very good with Char Sui Pork (p. 98) too. There are as many variations of *Nam Prik* as there are cooks in Thailand. This is the one used by our servants and cherished by some of our friends. Unfortunately, *Nam Prik* breath, which lasts until the next day, is a fearsome thing. You have been warned, but, believe us, the amazing taste is well worth the anti-social penalty.

INGREDIENTS

1 tablespoon dried shrimp	2 to 3 tablespoons jaggery (palm sugar) or brown sugar
2 teaspoons *blachan* (shrimp paste)	
3 garlic cloves	1/3 cup chopped fresh red chiles
3 ginger slices, peeled	1 teaspoon water
1 1/2 tablespoons lemon juice	1 teaspoon salt
1 tablespoon soy sauce	

METHOD

■ Soak the dried shrimp in water for 15 minutes, then rinse and drain.

■ Wrap the *blachan* in a little foil, and grill for 1 minute on each side.

■ Pound the garlic and ginger and shrimp together, then add the *blachan* and finally the rest of the ingredients. Alternatively, put the whole lot in a blender and process for a few minutes.

■ Serve with great caution—but bliss!

Sambol Ulek

INDONESIAN CHILE PASTE

SERVES 4

This is scorchingly hot so eat it in very small quantities! *Sambol Ulek* is wonderful stirred into other dishes to add just that extra bit of fire. Keep it in an airtight jar in the refrigerator and it will last for several weeks.

INGREDIENTS

20 fresh red chiles	2/3 cup rice wine vinegar
1 teaspoon salt	

METHOD

- Process the ingredients in a blender until smooth. Use with immense caution as a relish.

VARIATION

The Thais have their own version of this using 8 red chiles and 6 tablespoons lime juice. This will keep for up to a week in the refrigerator.

Vietnamese Dipping Sauce

SERVES 4 TO 6

Lovely to use as a dipping sauce for Stuffed Spring Rolls (p. 48) or just to spice up any dish instead of ordinary soy sauce. This sauce is only faintly fishy—more sweet, sour, and hot—and quite delicate, even with the garlic.

INGREDIENTS

1/2 cup fish sauce	2 fresh red chiles
2 garlic cloves, crushed	1 tablespoon sugar
Juice and flesh of 2 lemons	

METHOD

- Put all the ingredients into a blender with 4 tablespoons water and blend for a few minutes. Serve in small bowls.

Tiger Lily's Special Sweet & Sour Sauce

This sauce is perfect for dipping or pouring over small pieces of meat, fish, or chicken, deep-fried in a crisp batter.

INGREDIENTS

1/2 cup tomato ketchup (preferably Heinz)	1 teaspoon fresh minced ginger
1 tablespoon rice wine vinegar	1 tablespoon crushed pineapple (canned in syrup is fine)
3 tablespoons sugar	
2 garlic cloves, crushed	1 tablespoon cornstarch, blended with 3 tablespoons water

METHOD

■ Combine all the ingredients in a saucepan except for the cornstarch mixture, add 1/2 cup water, and bring to a boil.

■ Add the cornstarch and bring to a boil again, stirring until the mixture thickens.

VARIATIONS

■ Try adding slices of bell peppers, onions, and carrots. Blanch any combination of these in boiling water, refresh immediately under cold water, and add to the hot sauce. Cook for a few minutes to let the flavors sink in, but not long enough to make the vegetables limp and flabby.

■ If desired, stir in some roasted cashew nuts and chunks of pineapple before serving.

■ To make the sauce spicy, add 1/2 to 1 teaspoon ground red pepper and/or 1 teaspoon Worcestershire sauce.

Quick Plum Sauce

MAKES ABOUT
2/3 CUP

If you have run out of hoisin or plum sauce, the stores are closed and your Peking duck and pancakes are ready to serve, you can always whip up a batch of this super-easy alternative. It is equally good as a dipping sauce for Wontons (page 43) or Stuffed Spring Rolls (page 48).

INGREDIENTS

1/2 cup plum or peach jam (look for the one with the highest fruit content)

2 tablespoons chutney

2 tablespoons rice wine vinegar

1/2 teaspoon ground red pepper (optional)

METHOD

▪ Place all the ingredients in a blender and process until smooth.

Satay Sauce

SERVES 6 TO 8

An essential sauce to accompany Satay (page 94) or the Indonesian vegetable salad, Gado Gado (page 144).

This recipe evolved from our desire to use what was freely available and cut down on time and effort, but not at the expense of taste. We would use fresh peanuts and grind them ourselves back home, but long live crunchy peanut butter from the supermarket!

When serving this sauce, remember to warn your guests that it contains peanuts in case anyone suffers from an allergic reaction.

INGREDIENTS

1 small onion, very finely chopped	1 tablespoon lime juice
2 garlic cloves, crushed	1 stalk lemongrass or grated rind of 1 lemon
2 fresh red chiles, chopped	1 teaspoon *blachan* (shrimp paste) wrapped in foil and broiled for 1 minute on each side (optional)
3 tablespoons vegetable oil	
2 teaspoons jaggery (palm sugar) or dark brown sugar	
1/2 teaspoon salt	2 cups coconut milk
2 tablespoons soy sauce	1 3/4 cups crunchy peanut butter
	1/2 teaspoon ground red pepper (optional)

METHOD

■ Fry the onion, garlic, and chiles in the oil until they begin to brown.

■ Add the jaggery, salt, soy sauce, lime juice, lemongrass, and *blachan*. Bring to a boil and simmer for 5 minutes.

■ Stir in the coconut milk and peanut butter and simmer until the sauce thickens and the oil just begins to separate.

■ Taste and adjust the seasoning, adding 1/2 teaspoon ground red pepper and more salt if desired. If the sauce is too thick, add a little extra hot water to thin it down.

Homemade Chicken Stock

Every Chinese cook will have a store of this stock in his or her refrigerator. If you remember to give it a good boil (at least 5 minutes on a high rolling boil) once a week, cool, then refrigerate it, the stock will last for up to 3 weeks. Most of our Chinese recipes call for anything from a tablespoon to several cups of this stock, so it is worth making your own if you have the time and the inclination. Alternatively, you could use Knorr chicken stock cubes which are very authentic and almost as good.

INGREDIENTS

4-pound chicken or the same weight in chicken wings (this is a good way to use those wing tips discarded when you make Chicken Batons, page 107)

1 tablespoon salt

METHOD

■ Clean the chicken, removing any yellow fat from the body cavity. Save this, melt it, and use for stir-fries or for cooking fabulous golden roast potatoes. Chicken fat (like all animal fats) is high in cholesterol but the taste is superb and you will not be eating enough to cause any permanent damage to your arteries.

■ Put the chicken into a very large pot with the salt, add 5 1/2 quarts water, and bring to a boil. Simmer for up to 3 hours or cook in a pressure cooker for 30 minutes.

■ Cool, strain, and store in an airtight container in the refrigerator. Alternatively, pour into ice-cube trays and freeze. When you need it, just pop a frozen cube into your dish. What could be simpler? Save the chicken meat for chicken rillettes—remove some of the skin and discard. Then use 2 forks to shred the flesh (and some skin), add salt and pepper, mix with a little melted butter and eat on toast. Simply delicious.

VARIATION

The Chinese love pork as much as chicken, so you may want to use pork bones instead of chicken. Remember to remove the fat, which will harden on the surface when the stock cools. You are after a clear, well-flavored stock.

ABOUT SAMBOLS

It is interesting to compare dishes from around the world. For instance, South American salsas—raw tomato, onion, and chiles whirled together in a food processor and brought to life with lemon juice and salt—give the taste buds a touch of excitement, just like Eastern sambols. Every meal in Sri Lanka is served with at least one sambol on the side. These can be enhanced by the more Western accompaniment of green salad leaves, adding freshness, color, texture, and vitamins to enliven the meal.

Coconut Sambol

SERVES 4

The island of Sri Lanka abounds with swaying rustling coconut palms and we make use of all its products. Its leaves are woven into mats and shelters; its nuts provide coconut flesh, milk, and oil; the husk gives *copra* to fill mattresses and provide gardening centers across the world with eco-friendly compost; its trunk is used for wood, carvings, furniture, and kindling. From birth, Sri Lankans use coconut oil to keep their skins soft and wrinkle-free and on their hair to ensure it remains shiny and dark. Oh, yes, and its juice can be fermented to produce a mind-blowing native moonshine called toddy.

You will find references to Coconut Sambol throughout this book. Not only can it be served with Rice (page 63), Hoppers (page 72), Mock Stringhoppers (page 86), and Coconut Rotis (page 74), it can also be stirred into fried rice or noodles, added to soups or curries as a thickener, fried with cooked meat, onions, and potatoes for an instant spicy dry curry, and even added to pancake batter, baked potatoes, or cheese on toast.

Eat it often but in modest amounts—it should be quite spicy.

INGREDIENTS

1 cup fresh or dried grated coconut	3 curry leaves
1 teaspoon salt	1 small piece *rampe* (pandanus), approximately 1 inch long
1 teaspoon ground red pepper	
2 teaspoons maldive fish or ground dried shrimp	1 medium onion, roughly chopped
	1 teaspoon lemon juice

METHOD

■ Mix 2 tablespoons boiling water into the coconut to moisten. If using dried coconut add another 2 tablespoons hot water.

■ Put the rest of the ingredients into a blender and process for a few seconds only. It should not become a paste.

■ Combine all the ingredients and serve with just about anything, at any time! Coconut sambol will last for up to 3 days in a refrigerator or can be frozen for up to 2 months. Freeze in small amounts, enough for one meal.

HOW TO USE FRESH COCONUT— IF YOU REALLY MUST!

■ Select a fresh-looking nut and shake it. You should be able to hear some water sloshing around. This is not the milk—you make that by squeezing the grated coconut flesh in hot water and straining it.

■ Hold the nut in the palm of your hand with the 3 "eyes" at the top. Use the blunt edge of a large cleaver (not the sharp blade) to tap gently all the way around its center. Imagine it is the world and you are creating the equator!

■ Sharply tap the nut with the knife. With practice, it should divide neatly into 2 halves.

■ In Sri Lanka, someone would grate the coconut using a fearsome implement similar to a giant serrated screwdriver with 5 heads. You can cheat by cutting off the thin brown skin and putting the white flesh into your food processor and processing for only a few seconds.

■ We strongly suggest you forget this and go for your store-bought package of dried coconut!

Tomato, Cucumber, & Onion Sambol

SERVES 4 TO 6

One very strange thing we noticed when we returned East after many years of living in the West, was the absence of the green ridged cucumbers we were so used to seeing and eating. Now we were faced with huge balloon-sized yellow cucumbers. We were told that, even if seeds from the green ones were planted, after a season or two they would mutate into the yellow ones. We never stayed long enough in one place to test this out, but it sounds plausible. Another odd feature of the yellow cucumbers was that you had to cut a slice off the end, wait until it oozed a little milky sap and rub this vigorously across the cut end. If you forgot, the whole cucumber would taste bitter. The skin was very coarse, so it had to be removed.

For this recipe try to get the tastiest possible tomatoes and onions. Turn resolutely away from out-of-season supermarket tomatoes.

INGREDIENTS

1 pound tomatoes	1/2 teaspoon sugar
1/2 cucumber	2 teaspoons rice wine vinegar, or lemon or lime juice
1 medium onion, finely chopped	
1 teaspoon salt	1 teaspoon ground red pepper

METHOD

■ Dice the tomatoes and cucumber and add to the rest of the ingredients.

■ Mix and serve, preferably in a glass dish.

■ This sambol can be prepared up to 5 hours in advance but it must be eaten on the same day.

VARIATION

The addition of a little Coconut Sambol (page 30) will give this dish an extra zip.

Seeni Sambol

SUGAR SAMBOL

SERVES 8

This is the other indispensable item on every Sri Lankan table. *Seeni Sambol* can be eaten with bread, Hoppers (page 72), Mock Stringhoppers (page 86), Rice (page 63)…the list is endless. It is the "Siamese twin" of our beloved Coconut Sambol (page 30), so do try it. This sambol will keep for up to 3 days in the refrigerator, but rarely lasts that long because it is so "more-ish." Even if cooking a meal for 4, do make up this quantity and keep the leftovers.

INGREDIENTS

18 tablespoons coconut or vegetable oil (but not olive oil)	8 curry leaves
1 pound onions, finely sliced	2 tablespoons white rice vinegar
4 ounces maldive fish or dried shrimp, pounded	2 inch piece cinnamon stick
1 1/2 tablespoons ground red pepper	Small piece ginger, peeled and crushed
2 teaspoons salt	1 teaspoon ground mixed spice or allspice
	2 tablespoons dried coconut
	1 tablespoon sugar

METHOD

■ Heat the oil in a heavy frying pan and cook the onions slowly, stirring occasionally, until they turn transparent and all the water evaporates. This can take 15 to 20 minutes.

■ When the onions begin to caramelize and turn a delicious golden brown (the smell is absolutely mouth-watering), add the rest of the ingredients, except for the sugar, and simmer for 5 to 10 minutes.

■ Keep stirring until all the liquid has evaporated and the oil starts to separate and rise to the top. Stir in the sugar.

■ Taste and adjust the seasoning, adding more salt and ground red pepper, if desired. The sambol should be hot, sweet, and savory.

Tamarind Chutney

MAKES 5 JARS

A spicy, sweet, and sour chutney that has a very unusual fruity flavor. We love this with cheese and French bread as well as with our rice and curries.

INGREDIENTS

1 pound tamarind block	4 garlic cloves, chopped
8 ounces chopped stoned dates (1 1/4 cups)	1-inch piece ginger, peeled and crushed
4 ounces sultanas (1 1/4 cups, not packed)	1/3 cup rice wine vinegar
1 tablespoon ground red pepper	2 teaspoons salt
1 teaspoon ground cinnamon	1/2 cup jaggery (palm sugar) or dark brown sugar, packed

METHOD

■ Soak the tamarind in hot water for about 15 minutes until soft. Mash the pulp and strain, keeping only the liquid.

■ Combine all the ingredients in a pan and cook over a low heat, stirring continuously, until the mixture has the consistency of jam.

■ Bottle in clean dry jars. This fruity chutney will keep for 6 months.

STARTERS

▲▲▲▲▲▲▲▲▲▲▲▲▲▲▲▲▲▲

This chapter is a collection of our favorite recipes, which mirrors our diverse background. Wontons, Shrimp Toasts, Fried Seaweed, and Stuffed Spring Rolls come from our Chinese heritage and the others from our Asian roots. Southeast Asians and Orientals, like the Sri Lankans, do not have traditional starters. Instead, all the dishes are placed together on the table at once and it is customary to help yourself to a little of everything. You will find many recipes elsewhere in the book that would also make ideal starters, if you feel the need to divide your meal into Western-style courses.

We have given you this choice of raitas, dips, *Chavada* and our beloved Onion Bhajii recipe for no other reason than that we love them! A good way to serve the dips is with small baskets filled with some or all of the following to use to scoop up the lovely flavors:

- Shrimp crackers

- Tortilla chips or potato chips

- Mini pappadoms or large ones carefully cut into strips before frying (they are far too delicate to cut after they are cooked)

- Raw vegetables, such as celery, cucumber, tomatoes, lettuce

- Strips of cooked meat or fish, dipped in a simple batter and deep-fried

- Chicken Batons

- French bread, Quick and Easy *Naan* Bread, *Roti Djala*, all made mini-sized or cut into manageable pieces

If you really must serve the dips as a starter, try cutting up a portion of Indonesian Grilled Spicy Chicken, nestle the chicken pieces on a bed of shredded lettuce, and serve instead of the usual tandoori chicken.

Onion Bhajiis

Whenever we are asked by friends to bring some nibbles along for parties, these are always the first to disappear.

Chickpea (also known as besan, gram, or channa) flour is a dream to use. Gluten-free, it sticks like concrete to raw meat, fish, etc., and, unlike breadcrumbs, doesn't have the annoying habit of falling off food when you fry it. It mixes with water to make a lump-free cream that is then flavored with spices.

Although the recipe below is for Onion Bhajiis, any partly cooked vegetable can be added, e.g., peas, potatoes, cauliflower florets, or whole baby mushrooms. Strips of meat (partly cooked in a microwave or steamed for a few minutes) can also be used, such as chicken, beef, fish, etc. They are then called *pakoras*.

Bhajiis and *pakoras* freeze well (up to 2 months). Defrost and heat for a short time in a microwave or oven when needed. They are particularly useful if you want to prepare party food in advance.

If you can't find besan flour anywhere, you can substitute pea flour from a health-food store, or make your own. Dry-roast 1 pound of chickpeas or yellow split peas in a heavy pan on top of the stove over a medium heat. Stir the peas constantly with a wooden spoon to prevent them burning. When lightly toasted, cool, then put the peas through an electric coffee grinder or blender on high speed until powdered. Sift, then store in an airtight container.

INGREDIENTS

2 cups chickpea flour	1 teaspoon turmeric
2 teaspoons ground cumin	1 teaspoon ground red pepper
2 teaspoons ground coriander	2 large onions, chopped, or 1 pound alternative ingredients suggested above (e.g. peas, potatoes, etc.)
2 teaspoons salt	
1 teaspoon ground black pepper	4 cups oil for deep frying

METHOD

■ Sift the flour into a deep bowl, add the dry ingredients and 14 tablespoons water, and mix vigorously with a wooden spoon until it becomes a smooth cream.

■ Add the onions, or alternative ingredients, and ensure they are well coated in batter.

■ Heat the oil in a wok or deep-fryer until it begins to smoke. A drop of batter will immediately rise to the surface and begin to turn brown when the oil is at the right temperature. Turn the heat down to medium heat.

■ Use either 2 teaspoons for cocktail-sized *bhajiis*, or 1 heaping tablespoon for larger ones, and scoop spoonfuls of batter into the oil. Use the second spoon to push it off the first so you get a uniform shape and size.

■ Fry a few at a time, turning them once. When they begin to turn brown, take them out with a slotted spoon and drain on crumpled paper towels.

■ Serve with a range of chutneys and yogurt dips.

VARIATION

For an even more special taste, add 1 tablespoon finely chopped fresh coriander (cilantro) leaves and/or 1 teaspoon mint sauce to the batter before adding the onions, etc.

ABOUT SPECIAL DIPS

Everyone's heart sinks when confronted by the obligatory tray of sad-looking cucumber, celery, and carrot sticks, usually served with some violent pink taramasalata and gray hummus, which pass for crudités or hors d'oeuvres at cocktail parties. Strange how this always seems to be the one tray that remains virtually untouched throughout, and ends up being swept into the garbage.

Instead, try batons of raw zucchini or turnip (use young ones that have not gone spongy), whole cherry tomatoes, boiled quail's eggs, and lightly steamed sticks of beets, snowpeas, or small green beans.

Slices of fresh peeled fruit, such as mangoes, peaches, nectarines, or pears, can also add a stunning visual contrast and interesting flavor but remember to go for freshness, crunch, and color. Add some Onion Bhajiis (page 36), pappadoms and mini pita breads or Coconut Rotis (page 74) and you have a substantial starter. Served with a Lentil Soup and bread, it becomes a balanced meal, just bursting with vitamins and taste.

So walk resolutely past the refrigerated section of supermarket dips and try making your own.

Mint and Yogurt Dip

SERVES 4

This dip is so simple we are almost embarrassed to include it. But it tastes so good and is as much at home partnered with Indonesian Grilled Spicy Chicken (page 112) as Onion Bhajiis (page 36) and pappadoms so we just had to share it with you. It is also very pretty—golden yellow with flecks of bright green. Strangely enough, the cheapest, most sugary, and vinegary supermarket brand mint sauce is the best for this recipe.

INGREDIENTS

1 1/3 cups plain yogurt (preferably the thick-set Greek type)

2 teaspoons ground turmeric

1/2 teaspoon salt

1/4 teaspoon ground red pepper

1/4 teaspoon ground coriander

1/4 teaspoon ground cumin

2 teaspoons mint sauce

Sugar, to taste

METHOD

■ Drain off any liquid from the yogurt, then place in a bowl and beat with a fork until smooth.

■ Add the remaining ingredients and blend well.

■ Serve in a pretty shallow bowl. If you are delicate by nature, and steady of hand, you can decorate the top of the bowl with concentric circles made from pinches of turmeric, cumin, coriander, and paprika. It does look wonderful!

Tamarind & Date Dip

SERVES 6

This is one of the easiest yet most scrumptious dips we have had the good fortune to encounter. Deep brown, hot, and spicy but deliciously sweet and sour, too.

We had an aunt with a tamarind tree in her garden and we just couldn't wait for the season to come around when we could gorge ourselves on the long papery pods with their deliciously sticky centers and dark shiny seeds, even though we usually suffered from tummy ache afterwards. Many animals shared our love of the fruit, and fruit bats, monkeys, and even elephants were occasionally sighted around the heavily laden tree.

Tamarind is used in the East as a preservative instead of vinegar and lemon juice. Its tart, sweet yet sour flavor is unsurpassed in curries and soups. Buy it in dark dried blocks of 1/2 to 1 pound weight. This dip is especially good with seafood or with traditional Peking Pancakes (page 82) and roast duck.

INGREDIENTS

8 ounces dried tamarind (seedless if possible)

1 1/4 cups chopped stoned dates

Juice of 2 limes or one tablespoon lemon juice

1 teaspoon salt

1 teaspoon ground cumin

1 teaspoon ground coriander

1 to 2 teaspoons ground red pepper

A few sesame seeds (optional)

METHOD

■ Break up the tamarind block and place it in a bowl. Boil 2 1/4 cups water, pour over the tamarind, and soak for 30 minutes.

■ Strain to remove the seeds (if any) and pith. Some tamarind blocks are more fibrous than others—don't be afraid to squeeze the pulp with well-washed hands like we do in the East.

■ Mix the strained liquid with all the other ingredients, except the sesame seeds, put in a saucepan, and simmer, uncovered, for about 15 minutes.

■ Cool, then strain again and purée. Place the thick sauce in a bowl and serve. If the sauce is too thick, add a little hot water to thin it down.

■ Sprinkle the sesame seeds on top of the dip, for contrast, if you wish.

Coconut, Coriander, & Chile Dip

SERVES 4

A beautiful pale green dip or sauce that will add color to your buffet table. It's excellent with *pakoras* (page 36) and Chicken Batons (page 107)

INGREDIENTS

8 ounces dried coconut (4 cups)	1 to 2 teaspoons salt
1/2 cup chopped fresh coriander (cilantro)	1 tablespoon sugar
4 fresh green chiles	1 tablespoon lemon juice

METHOD

■ Put all the ingredients in a blender or food processor with 1/2 cup water and process until smooth. Leave to stand for an hour for the flavors to develop.

■ Serve in a shallow bowl, or use a halved melon (remove some of the flesh and all of the seeds) as a container and scatter a few edible flower petals on top. Try nasturtiums or marigolds.

Tomato, Garlic, & Chile Dip

SERVES 4

This spicy, sweet tomato dip with undertones of garlic is very good with strips of chicken or fish dipped in batter and fried, or with freshly boiled shrimp.

Heinz tomato ketchup is made with tomatoes, spices, and little else, and is hard to beat as the tomato base for many of our sweet-and-sour recipes. If you can find an equal, then use it by all means—but read the label carefully and please shun any that contain flour or thickeners.

INGREDIENTS

4 tablespoons tomato ketchup	1 teaspoon salt
1 tablespoon rice wine vinegar	2 teaspoons ground red pepper
3 garlic cloves, very finely minced	

METHOD

■ Put all the ingredients in a saucepan with 4 tablespoons water and simmer for 5 to 10 minutes.

■ Cool, then purée and serve in a shallow bowl. If you can get hold of a giant beef tomato, you can cut the top off, scoop out the inside and serve the dip in it.

Banana Raita

SERVES 6 TO 8

Everyone must have eaten cucumber raita in an Indian restaurant. Mild, cooling, and creamy, it helps to put out the fire of a too-hot curry. Why not try our fruit alternatives for a change? The sweetness is quite unusual. Do experiment with other fruit in season. Summer fruit could be equally pleasing—try adding raspberries, strawberries, or even black currants or elderberries.

INGREDIENTS

2 cups thick-set yogurt	1/2 teaspoon ground coriander
4 bananas, peeled, sliced, and mixed with 1 tablespoon lemon juice	1/2 teaspoon ground cumin
2 green chiles, finely chopped	1/2 teaspoon salt

METHOD

■ Drain off any liquid from the yogurt, then place in a bowl and beat with a fork until smooth.

■ Add the remaining ingredients and blend well. Cover with plastic wrap and refrigerate until needed. This dish does not keep well, so it's best eaten the same day.

VARIATIONS

■ Sprinkle 2 teaspoons chopped coriander leaves (cilantro) over as a garnish before serving.

■ Replace the bananas with one of the following: 1/2 cup peeled, chopped, and drained pineapple, peaches, or kiwi fruit.

ABOUT WONTONS

Wontons are Chinese ravioli that are boiled and served in soup or deep-fried and served with a range of dipping sauces. We know they are fattening when deep-fried and we should really steer clear of them but, oh, they are such a temptation…!

Wonton skins are little squares of egg-and-flour dough and they are readily available from Chinese specialty shops. If you cannot track them down, you can use filo pastry or make your own noodle dough and just roll it out very thinly before cutting it into 2-inch squares or rounds. Your wontons may not look ultra-elegant, but they will still taste wonderful.

The recipes for fillings will each make 25 to 40 wontons, enough to serve 6 to 8 people. You can use any of these recipes but do not over-fill your wontons or they will burst. This is how to fill them:

■ Put a very small amount of filling (about 1/2 teaspoon) in the middle of a square of dough. For folded wontons (see **a.** below), fold in half to make a triangle. Pinch the open sides together to seal, using a little water if necessary to make them stick. Fold the right and then the left corner up to the center. Pinch together. For money-bag wontons (see **b.** below), bring all four corners together like a triangle. Dampen around the filling, with a little beaten egg, and press firmly to seal. There should be a frill of wonton pastry around the edge. Part of the pleasure of eating wontons is crunching through these frills.

■ Place the wontons on a lightly floured plate until ready to cook (see page 45).

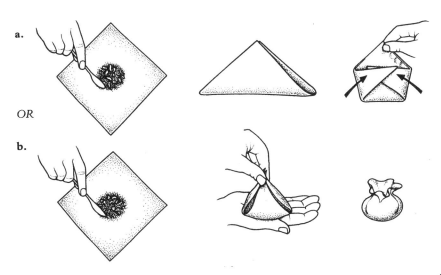

a.

OR

b.

Whole Shrimp Filling

SERVES 6 TO 8

Use uncooked raw shrimp for the best results or else cooked shrimp with their shells on.

INGREDIENTS

1 pound shrimp	Salt and pepper

METHOD

■ Peel the shrimp and remove the heads and black lines running down their backs (the intestinal tract).

■ Put a cleaned shrimp in the center of each wonton skin. Sprinkle with a little salt and pepper. Seal as described on page 43.

Pork Filling

SERVES 6 TO 8

Either use ground pork (make your own from any cut but discard any sinews and skin before chopping in a food processor, taking care not to over-process) or use best-quality pork sausage. If using the sausage, make a slit down one side, remove the meat, and throw away the skin. Choose a chunky-cut sausage. You do not want a paste, but a rather rough texture.

INGREDIENTS

8 ounces ground pork or pork sausage	1/2 teaspoon sweet sherry
1/2 teaspoon cornstarch	1/2 teaspoon soy sauce
1/4 teaspoon salt	2 tablespoons chopped canned water chestnuts

METHOD

■ Mix all the ingredients together and use to fill wonton skins as described on page 43.

Crab & Cheese Filling

SERVES 6 TO 8

INGREDIENTS

1 (6-ounce) can crabmeat	1/4 teaspoon ground black pepper
3 ounces cream cheese	2 scallions, trimmed and finely chopped
1/2 teaspoon hoisin sauce	

METHOD

■ Mix the ingredients and fill wonton skins as described on page 43.

VARIATION

Try adding 2 tablespoons chopped watercress or 1 tablespoon very finely chopped celery. The first makes this filling delightfully peppery.

COOKING THE WONTONS

For fried wontons, deep-fry them in hot oil a few at a time. Remove with a slotted spoon when crispy and brown and drain on paper towels. Serve hot with Tiger Lily's Special Sweet & Sour Sauce (page 26).

For boiled wontons, dissolve 2 good-quality chicken stock cubes in 3 1/2 cups water, or use the same quantity of Homemade Chicken Stock (page 29). Bring to a boil and drop in the wontons. They are cooked when they float to the surface (about 5 minutes). Wash a bunch of watercress or a cup of shredded spinach or greens. Add to the soup. Bring to a boil for 2 minutes, and serve with soy sauce and a good chile sauce.

Shrimp Toasts

SERVES 6 TO 8
AS A STARTER

We use leftover white supermarket bread that is going stale to make this impressive appetizer.

INGREDIENTS

8 ounces peeled shrimp	2 tablespoons cornstarch
2 tablespoons ground pork or meat from 1 good-quality pork sausage	12 to 15 slices thinly sliced white bread
1 tablespoon sherry	1 egg, lightly beaten
2 medium egg whites, beaten until stiff	4 cups oil for deep-frying

METHOD

■ Place the shrimp, pork, sherry, egg whites, and half the cornstarch in a blender and blend to a thick paste.

■ Cut the bread into fingers or triangles, or stamp out into pretty shapes with cutters. Beat the leftover cornstarch with the whole egg and brush the mixture over the pieces of bread.

■ Spread the shrimp paste over the bread shapes, then deep-fry in hot oil until golden, a few at a time, shrimp side down.

■ Turn after a few minutes and fry on the other side until golden.

■ Remove from the oil with a slotted spoon and drain on paper towels. Serve hot with Quick Plum Sauce (page 27) or Tamarind & Date Dip (page 40).

VARIATIONS

■ Try adding a sprinkling of chopped coriander (cilantro) leaves and/or 1 finely chopped chile before you spread the paste on the bread shapes.

■ Crush 1 small clove of garlic and a little ginger together and add to the paste.

■ 1 teaspoon sesame oil added to the paste, with a small amount of lime juice, gives it a Thai flavor.

■ Sprinkle sesame seeds over the toast before frying, and press in lightly.

Fried "Seaweed"

SERVES 4

We love the crisp, almost cellophane texture of this dish, and its deep green color. Using coarse-ground sea salt to season it brings back memories of the sea. Of course it isn't really seaweed—so don't be put off trying this surprisingly easy recipe. We serve it as a garnish for wontons with our Special Sweet & Sour Sauce (page 26) for a really stunning starter.

Just take care not to burn the seaweed. Cook it in very small batches, watch it like a hawk when it hits the hot oil and remove it as soon as it looks crisp. It will only take a few seconds. Take care to dry the leaves thoroughly on a kitchen towel before frying, as any water will make the hot oil splatter.

INGREDIENTS

1 pound spring greens or cauliflower leaves, washed and dried thoroughly	Sea salt or a pinch of ground dried shrimp for sprinkling
1 1/4 cups oil for deep-frying	

METHOD

■ Gather a few leaves together, roll into a cigar shape and, using a very sharp knife, cut into very thin shreds. Repeat with other leaves.

■ Heat the oil in a wok or deep-fryer. When almost smoking, add a handful of shreds and immediately begin to turn them with a slotted spoon.

■ Keep turning and moving around for a few seconds, then lift out and drain on paper towels. The seaweed should be crisp and bright green in color. Sprinkle with a little sea salt or ground dried shrimp and serve.

Stuffed Spring Rolls

SERVES 4 TO 6

Either use store-bought wonton wrappers or make your own Peking Pancakes or Spring Roll Wrappers (page 82). Everyone has a favorite recipe for these popular starters, but we love this one especially. This makes between 12 and 24 rolls, depending on the size. Tiny ones, the size of a baby's finger, are too enticing to be left alone, and well worth the initial effort.

Any leftover stir-fried dishes can be used up as spring roll fillings as long as they are not too liquid. You can thicken them by adding a little cornstarch, then boiling if necessary. Taste and adjust the seasoning—the filling should be highly flavored to contrast with the bland wrapper.

INGREDIENTS

1 (7-ounce) can bamboo shoots	1/2 cup shelled and chopped shrimp
1 medium carrot, peeled	1/2 teaspoon sugar
2 celery stalks, washed and trimmed	1/2 teaspoon *Sambol Ulek* (page 25)
1 teaspoon vegetable oil	1 teaspoon cornstarch, mixed with 1 teaspoon sherry
1 garlic clove, crushed	
3 scallions, washed, trimmed, and finely chopped (optional)	1 egg, beaten
	1 1/4 cups oil for deep-frying
1/2 cup bean sprouts	

METHOD

■ Drain the bamboo shoots, then cut into very fine shreds. Cut the carrot and celery into thin strips.

■ Heat 1 teaspoon vegetable oil in a wok. When it begins to smoke, add the garlic and vegetables and stir-fry for a few seconds only.

■ Lastly, add the shrimps, sugar, *Sambol Ulek*, and cornstarch mixture and stir for a few seconds more. Do not overcook, as the rolls will be fried again later. Put the filling aside to cool.

■ Take a wrapper, and place it on a floured surface. Cover the others so they do not dry out. Put about 2 teaspoons filling for the smaller rolls, and a tablespoon for the larger ones, at one end of each wrapper and fold the sides in. (See diagrams opposite.)

■ Brush the sides with beaten egg and roll firmly into cigar shapes. Take care to use plenty of egg and seal the ends properly.

■ Heat the oil in a wok or deep-fryer and cook the rolls until they are golden brown. Drain on paper towels and serve hot.

■ Sauces recommended to accompany this recipe are *Nam Prik* (page 24), Tamarind & Date Dip (page 40) or this special fish sauce: mix together 1 teaspoon *Sambol Ulek* (page 25) with 1/2 teaspoon *Balichaw* (page 23), 1 table-spoon fish sauce, 1 teaspoon sugar, and 1 tablespoon rice wine vinegar.

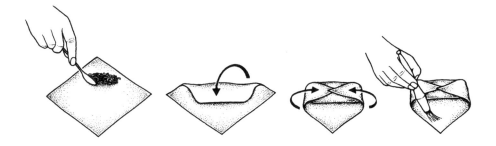

Chavada

BOMBAY MIX

SERVES
10 TO 12

*C*havada is simple to prepare. It can be kept fresh for up to 5 weeks in an airtight container. Be sure *not* to make this in bulk, because the temptation to eat a lot of it will be too strong to resist and your waistline will not thank you!

INGREDIENTS

1 pound dried *channa dhal* or chickpeas	3/4 cup sultanas (optional)
2 1/4 cups oil for deep-frying	2 teaspoons salt
8 ounces Rice Krispies (yes, the kiddies' favorite breakfast cereal!) (8 cups)	1 teaspoon ground turmeric
Roasted salted peanuts (1 1/2 cups)	1 teaspoon ground red pepper
8 ounces potato chips broken into smallish pieces (200 chips)	

METHOD

■ Put the *channa* or chickpeas in a deep bowl and cover with at least 8 cups water. Leave to soak overnight, after which they will have almost doubled in size.

■ Drain the chickpeas, then spread them out on a clean kitchen towel, and allow to dry for about an hour.

■ Bring the oil up to smoking point in a wok or deep-fryer, lower the heat, and fry small quantities of chickpeas until golden brown. Eat one—it should be crunchy but not too hard.

■ Lift the chickpeas out of the oil with a slotted spoon and allow to dry on paper towels.

■ Fry handfuls of the puffed rice in the same oil but watch carefully. They need only a few seconds and will burn quite easily if not taken out almost immediately. Dry on more paper towels.

■ Put all the ingredients into a bowl and mix thoroughly. Taste and adjust the seasoning, adding more red pepper or salt if desired. Store in an airtight container.

VARIATION

Add 8 ounces (1 2/3 cups) salted cashew nuts.

SOUPS

▲▲▲▲▲▲▲▲▲▲▲▲▲▲▲▲

This chapter includes a wide range of tastes and flavors, sweeping across Southeast Asian cuisine like a giant paintbrush.

Hodi sits rather uncomfortably here, as it is not strictly a soup. It would never be served on its own but as a "wetting agent" for dry dishes like Coconut Rotis, Mock Stringhoppers, or even plain rice. *Hodi* and *Rasam* can act as bases for unusual curries. *Hodi* creates mild "white" curry while *Rasam*'s fiery, acidic taste peps up a hot curry. Simply slice vegetables or meat and boil or simmer them until tender in the chosen liquid, seasoning as required with extra chiles and other ingredients.

We include here everybody's favorites: like Mulligatawny, beloved of ex-pats who still yearn for the days of the Raj; Thailand's hot *Tom Yum Kung* with its sharp mix of shrimp, lemongrass, and chiles; and China's ever-popular Egg Drop Soup.

We have eaten in restaurants across the world and are sometimes disappointed, particularly in the suburbs, when cooks alter recipes supposedly to suit Western palates. This usually means cutting down on the seasoning, and bumping up the liquid, while overdosing on cornstarch and the dreaded monosodium glutamate.

If eating out, we always choose the ethnic quarter of any large city and are often to be found with our noses pressed up against steamy windows checking out the diners. If a Chinese restaurant is packed with Chinese that is our cue to enter and feast!

Tastes differ so we have tried to steer a middle course in our recipes—be generous with the extra seasoning if you like it that way, or add more water if you find the flavors too strong.

Lentil Soup

SERVES 6 TO 8

This deliciously creamy soup is not fiery hot, just pleasantly spicy. Do try it.

INGREDIENTS

1 1/4 cups lentils (any type—we use the ordinary red ones most often)	1 teaspoon ground cumin
3 carrots, chopped	3 teaspoons salt
3 large onions, chopped	4 curry leaves (optional)
1 celery stalk, washed, trimmed, and chopped	1/2 cup coconut milk
3 garlic cloves, crushed	2 teaspoons lime or lemon juice
2 teaspoons black peppercorns, freshly ground	1 teaspoon Garam Masala (page 18)

METHOD

■ Wash the lentils in several changes of water. Place in a large saucepan with all the ingredients, except the coconut milk, lime or lemon juice, and Garam Masala. Add 6 cups water, bring to a boil, then reduce the heat and simmer for 30 minutes or until all the vegetables are tender.

■ Put the soup through a food mill, return to the pan, and add the coconut milk and lime or lemon juice. Stir in the Garam Masala, adjust the seasoning, and serve with lots of hot crusty bread or with rice and curry.

VARIATION

Try adding 1/4 to 1/2 teaspoon Thai Red or Green Curry Paste 2 (pages 20–21) to the soup just before serving. Stir well.

Chinese Chicken & Mushroom Soup

SERVES 4 TO 6

It makes us very happy that there are so many types of mushrooms flooding the market! Our favorites are fresh oyster, ordinary white buttons, canned straw, and dried wood ear. These last Chinese specialty mushrooms look like tiny brittle frills of black satin. Soak for 1 to 2 hours, then carefully strain off any impurities and use the mushrooms and their soaking water to add a delightful crunchy texture, rich flavor, and color contrast to any dish. They might seem expensive, but you only use a few at a time and they seem to last forever.

INGREDIENTS

8 ounces boneless skinless chicken breast	4 ounces mixed mushrooms, drained if canned, sliced or quartered depending on size and shape
5 cups Homemade Chicken Stock (page 29), or 2 good-quality chicken stock cubes dissolved in the same quantity of water	1/2 teaspoon ground white pepper
	1/2 teaspoon sugar
	2 scallions, washed, trimmed, and chopped

METHOD

■ Slice the chicken breast into long, thin slivers with a very sharp knife and set aside.

■ Put the chicken stock into a saucepan and bring to a boil.

■ Add the mushrooms and boil for only 3 minutes. Then add the chicken, pepper, and sugar and boil for another 3 minutes or until the meat turns opaque. Do not overcook.

■ Scatter the chopped scallions over the soup and serve.

VARIATIONS

■ Stir 1 teaspoon sesame oil into the finished soup.

■ If a spicier flavor is desired, try adding any one of our Thai Curry Pastes (pages 20–21) but in very small quantities (only 1/8 teaspoon). This soup is meant to be delicate.

Hot Sour Soup

SERVES 4

A uniquely tangy soup. We took Justin's (Rani's eldest son's) girlfriend, Caroline, out for one of our innumerable family dinners in Soho. It was the first time she had met us *en masse* and, being the exquisitely polite girl she is, she ate a little of everything rather than offend. Justin had ordered his favorite, fiery Hot Sour Soup—Caroline is very fair and turned nearly puce when she tried it!

Tofu, or bean curd, is found in many shops now. Very nutritious, it is delicate and needs gentle handling. Strain off the water it is stored in, then cut into cubes. Tofu can also be deep-fried and drained on paper towels. It has no taste of its own, but soaks up the flavor of whatever it is added to.

INGREDIENTS

2 1/4 cups Homemade Chicken Stock (page 29) or 1 chicken stock cube dissolved in the same quantity of water	4 ounces cooked sliced chicken (1 cup)
	2 ounces sliced canned bamboo shoots
2 tablespoons rice wine vinegar	2 ounces water chestnuts
1/2 teaspoon salt	2 ounces dried wood ear mushrooms, soaked and sliced (add liquid to the soup)
1/2 teaspoon ground white pepper	
1 teaspoon Thai Green Curry Paste 1 (page 21)	1/4 cup diced tofu
	1/4 cup frozen garden peas
3 tablespoons cornstarch, mixed to a cream with 3 tablespoons water	1 tablespoon soy sauce

METHOD

■ Put the chicken stock, vinegar, salt, pepper, and curry paste into a saucepan and bring to a boil.

■ Add the cornstarch mixture and stir until it begins to thicken. Lower the heat, add the rest of the ingredients, and heat through. Take care not to break up the cubes of tofu when serving.

VARIATION

If desired, a teaspoon each of sherry and sesame seed oil can be added before serving.

Hodi

COCONUT MILK SOUP

SERVES 4

Although not strictly a soup, this Sri Lankan specialty is made by every household almost daily. It is usually poured over stringhoppers (rice noodles), steamed lacy pancakes made of rice flour, or *pittu*—a savory made with fresh coconut, and flour, steamed in a hollow bamboo and sliced to eat with curry.

We had to improvise when we arrived in the West and found that many of the foods we loved were no longer available. This is a simplified recipe we devised. Do not boil; warm it gently or it will curdle.

A variety of vegetables, shellfish, and even diced meat can be included to make a mild "white" curry. You can add heat if you wish with a teaspoon of Thai Red or Green Curry Paste 2 (pages 20–21) or *Balichaw* (page 23).

Although the optional ingredients add the truly authentic flavor, the soup tastes just as good without them.

INGREDIENTS

2 1/4 cups Homemade Chicken Stock (page 29), or 1 chicken or vegetable stock cube dissolved in the same quantity of water	1/2 teaspoon ground cinnamon
	2 small green chiles, chopped
	1 teaspoon grated maldive fish, salted fish, or dried shrimp (optional)
1 medium onion, chopped	4 curry leaves (optional)
1 garlic clove, crushed	1-inch piece *rampe* or pandanus (optional)
1/2 teaspoon ground turmeric	2/3 cup coconut milk
1 teaspoon salt	1 tablespoon lemon juice

METHOD

■ Put the stock in a saucepan and add all the ingredients except for the coconut milk and lemon juice. Cook over a medium heat until the onion is tender.

■ Add the coconut milk and stir to dissolve. At the point of serving, add the lemon juice and stir again.

Mulligatawny

SERVES 4 TO 6

There are as many recipes for Mulligatawny as there are for Cornish pasties. Some are elaborate and call for endless ingredients, while others are fairly simple. We hope the recipe below will become one of your favorites.

INGREDIENTS

1 pound stewing beef, cut into approximately 1/2-inch cubes	2 teaspoons ground coriander
	1/4 teaspoon ground turmeric
1 pound soup bones (ask the butcher to chop these into small pieces)	2 teaspoons salt
	1 medium onion, sliced
2 medium onions, diced	1 tablespoon vegetable oil
2 tablespoons very finely sliced ginger	8 ounces potatoes, peeled and cut into very small dice
6 garlic cloves, crushed	
16 black peppercorns	1/3 cup coconut milk
1 teaspoon ground cumin	1 tablespoon lemon or lime juice

METHOD

■ Combine the beef, bones, diced onions and seasonings in a large saucepan. Add 7 cups water, bring to a boil, and skim off any froth. Reduce the heat, cover, and simmer for 2 hours (or 15 minutes in a pressure cooker).

■ Strain the stock, saving the diced onions and pieces of meat.

■ Fry the sliced onion in the oil, add the meat, diced onions, and the potatoes, and stir-fry until just turning brown.

■ Return the stock to the saucepan or pressure cooker, add the onion mixture, and bring to a boil. Simmer for about 10 minutes or until the potatoes are just cooked.

■ Add the coconut milk and lemon or lime juice just before serving. Take care not to boil the soup again, or it may curdle.

VARIATION

Like most Sri Lankan or Asian side dishes, this one is improved by the addition of a 2-inch piece of pandamus (rampe) leaf or 4 curry leaves to the stock. Although not essential, they impart a delicious flavor.

Rasam

PEPPER WATER

SERVES 4

Originating in India, *Rasam* is a thin acidic soup, very peppery and hot, which is drunk during the main meal or poured over dry rice and curries. Many believe it stops the pain of indigestion—and hangovers! It is excellent for cutting through the richness of many curries.

INGREDIENTS

2 ounces dried tamarind (about 3 table-spoons)	1 teaspoon salt
	1 teaspoon ground cumin
12 black peppercorns (or 2 teaspoons ground black pepper but make sure it is fresh)	2 teaspoons vegetable oil
	2 teaspoons whole mustard seeds, slightly crushed
1/2 medium onion	
2 garlic cloves, crushed	3 curry leaves (optional)

METHOD

■ Pour 2 1/4 cups hot water over the tamarind and leave it to soak. When cool, strain to remove the seeds and any pith.

■ Crush the peppercorns and chop the onion finely. Put all the ingredients, except the oil, mustard seeds, and curry leaves, in a saucepan and bring to a boil. Turn the heat down and simmer for 15 minutes.

■ Put the oil in a frying pan and, when hot, add the mustard seeds (and curry leaves if using). When the seeds pop, remove the pan from the heat, add the contents of the other saucepan, and serve.

VARIATION

If desired, add 2 tablespoons red lentils and 1 tablespoon diced raw potato with the onions. Boil the *Rasam* until they are cooked, adding more water if necessary.

Egg Drop Soup

SERVES 4

You will come across different versions of Egg Drop Soup in every Chinese restaurant across the globe. Once you know how easy it is to prepare, you can let your imagination run riot by adding all sorts of ingredients (see Variations, below). Unlike the clear soups usually served in Thailand and Indonesia, this one has a thickened base so it is more substantial.

When cooking for a dinner party, prepare the soup up to step 2 and set aside. Then you need only allow 3 minutes for step 3 onwards—what could be easier or quicker?

INGREDIENTS

4 cups Homemade Chicken Stock or 2 good chicken or vegetable stock cubes dissolved in the same quantity of water	2 eggs, lightly beaten
	3 scallions, washed, trimmed, and finely chopped
1 slice (about 1 teaspoon) ginger, cut into very fine slivers	1 teaspoon sherry or ginger wine to taste
	1/8 teaspoon ground white pepper
1 tablespoon cornstarch, mixed to a cream with 2 tablespoons water	Salt (optional)

METHOD

■ Put the stock and ginger into a large saucepan and bring to a boil. Simmer for 10 minutes, then check the seasoning, and adjust if necessary.

■ Slowly pour in the cornstarch mixture, stirring well. Boil until the soup becomes clear and thickens.

■ Add the beaten eggs, stirring well, and take off the heat. The eggs should begin to form strands in the soup.

■ Add the scallions, sherry or ginger wine, and pepper; taste and add salt if needed.

■ Serve immediately. This soup cannot be reheated.

VARIATION

■ Add 1/2 to 1 cup shredded crabmeat.

■ Add 1 cup each: shredded cooked chicken and cucumber pieces; or shredded ham and lettuce; or 1/2 can creamed corn and chopped cooked chicken breast; or any variation of diced ham, meat, fish, or seafood.

Tom Yum Kung

SPICY SHRIMP & LEMON SOUP

SERVES 6 TO 8

This clear Thai soup has its cousin in nearly every country that borders the Pacific. Its wonderful contrasting hot and sour flavors reflect the best of Southeast Asian cuisine. If you can take it hotter, by all means add more hot peppers, but do take care! We have given double the normal recipe because we know you will want to save some for the freezer.

INGREDIENTS

2 pounds large shrimp in their shells

1 stalk lemongrass, chopped, or 1 teaspoon grated lime or lemon rind

1/4 teaspoon grated galangal or ginger

2 fresh red hot peppers, chopped

1 tablespoon fish sauce

2 to 3 tablespoons lime or lemon juice (try the smaller amount first, adding more to taste if necessary)

3 scallions, washed, trimmed, and chopped

2 tablespoons chopped cilantro leaves

METHOD

■ Remove the shells and heads from the shrimp. Save the meat.

■ Put the shells, heads, 7 cups water, and all the ingredients, except the shrimp meat, scallions, and cilantro leaves, into a large saucepan and bring to a boil.

■ Simmer for 10 minutes, then strain the stock.

■ Wash out the saucepan, return the stock to it, bring to a boil, and add the shrimp.

■ Warm the soup through, then just before serving, add the scallions and cilantro leaves. Taste and adjust the seasoning.

VARIATIONS

■ If you can get hold of 2 kaffir lime leaves, add these to the stock with the shrimp shells. They really do bring out the citrus flavor.

■ Add some *Sambol Ulek* (page 25) if you want to zap your taste buds well and truly!

Mixed Vegetable & Wonton Soup

SERVES 4 TO 5

This clear broth, served with either wontons or meatballs, is one of our easiest and most delicious soup recipes. It is also the one more requested by our family and friends. Needless to say, we don't mind preparing it because it is so easy and gives us more time to escape from the kitchen and chat with our loved ones.

This is a very substantial soup that can make a light lunch or supper dish on its own.

INGREDIENTS

20 Wontons (page 43) or 2 large premium sausages taken out of their skins and 1 tablespoon cornstarch

5 cups Homemade Chicken Stock (page 29) or 2 good chicken stock cubes dissolved in the same quantity of water

2 teaspoons soy sauce

1 teaspoon sherry

1/4 large cucumber, cut into very fine matchsticks

1 cup mixed sliced vegetables (this is an ideal way to use up any leftovers from previous recipes, e.g., use water chestnuts, mushrooms, and bamboo shoots)

1 ounce vermicelli or cellophane noodles, cut with scissors into 2-inch lengths and soaked in water

1/8 teaspoon ground white pepper

METHOD

■ If using the Wontons, prepare them and set aside. If using the pork balls, form the sausage meat into very small balls and roll them in the cornstarch to prevent them sticking together. Set aside.

■ Put the stock, soy sauce, and sherry in a large saucepan and bring to a boil.

■ Add the cucumber and mixed vegetables and boil for 1 minute.

■ Add the vermicelli and Wontons or pork balls and boil for another 2 minutes or until the Wontons or pork balls rise to the surface.

■ Stir in the pepper and serve immediately.

VARIATIONS

■ Sprinkle with 1 chopped scallion.

■ If you can get it, 1/2 teaspoon *tung choi* (preserved Chinese vegetable) adds a real boost—stir it in at the end.

Melon with Chicken & Ham

SERVES 6

Use Chinese winter melon if available, or young summer squash, seeded cucumbers, or even the white flesh between the rind and red flesh of watermelon. When we were small, Mum would cut the red flesh off the melon, give it to us in bowls and save the prized white flesh. We weren't trusted with the normal slices on the rind because we would invariably forget, and eat the juicy flesh right down to the green skin. Besides using it in this soup, she would cut the white melon flesh into small dice and stir-fry it with strips of pork, onions, and chiles in soy sauce—absolutely scrumptious!

This is a basic Vietnamese soup but similar dishes are found in Chinese, Japanese, and other Asian cuisines.

INGREDIENTS

1 pound chicken (on the bone and cut into small serving pieces)	2 pounds winter melon (or see above for variations), peeled, sliced, and cut into small chunks (use only the firm flesh—discard any spongy bits and the seeds)
6 scallions, washed, trimmed, and chopped	
1/2 teaspoon ground black pepper	1 tablespoon fish sauce
7 cups Homemade Chicken Stock (page 29) or water	4 ounces ham, cut into quite small, but thick, matchsticks
	1 teaspoon salt

METHOD

■ Put the chicken, scallions, pepper, and stock or water into a large saucepan and bring to a boil.

■ Cover and simmer for 1 hour (or 15 minutes in a pressure cooker).

■ Add the melon, fish sauce, ham, and salt, and boil for 1 minute only. Taste, adjust the seasoning, and serve.

VARIATIONS

■ We confess to using our good old standby, 3 chicken stock cubes with 1 teaspoon *tung choi* (preserved Chinese vegetable) instead of making our own stock when pushed for time. It still tastes delicious!

■ If you wish, you can substitute the same weight of pork or stewing beef for the chicken.

RICE

▲▲▲▲▲▲▲▲▲▲▲▲▲▲▲▲▲

COOKING RICE

There are a number of different rices in the East: white long-grain (Patna) and basmati are well known, and Thai fragrant rice is appearing on more dining tables. But what about trying unmilled red or country rice, or highly desirable small-grained samba, for a change? Most of these unusual rices absorb more water than ordinary Western rices—some of them up to double the quantity.

We prepare rice in the traditional manner—washing the grains under plenty of fresh running water until the water thrown away runs clear (this ensures the starch is rinsed out—along with the vitamins, alas, but this is how we do it back home).

To cook long-grain rice, put the rice in a saucepan, and add enough water to cover. Next, point your index finger directly at the rice, rest the finger at right angles to the surface and add enough water to reach the second joint of your finger. Bring the rice to a boil and boil fiercely until most of the water has evaporated (about 10 to 15 minutes) and little volcanoes of escaping steam blow bubbles on the surface. Immediately cover with a tight-fitting lid, lower the heat, and simmer for 10 minutes. Then turn the heat off and let the rice absorb and moisture by leaving it to rest for 10 minutes.

To cook small-grained rice, like samba, the water should come up to the knuckle.

The best way to ensure separate fluffy grains of rice every time is to invest in an electric rice cooker. You can pick them up for about $30 and, once you have one, you will really wonder how you ever managed without it. If you like trouble-free entertaining or just want a foolproof way to cook rice, there is no better piece of equipment to invest in. Every Asian family owns one—and most of them have a simple keep-warm feature, which is ideal for staggered meals when the family comes in at different times.

Yellow Rice

SERVES 4 TO 6

A large platter of saffron-flavored yellow rice is the centerpiece of any Sri Lankan party. Put the rice on a large oval platter and decorate with quartered hard-boiled eggs. Sprinkle over golden fried onions, salted cashew nuts, sultanas, and peas and serve.

INGREDIENTS

1/2 cup butter or ghee	1/2 cup coconut milk
A few strands of saffron soaked in a little warm milk or 2 tablespoons ground turmeric	2 1/4 cups Homemade Chicken Stock (page 29) or 2 good chicken or vegetable stock cubes dissolved in the same quantity of hot water
4 cloves	
2-inch piece of cinnamon stick	GARNISH
5 green cardamom pods, bruised	4 eggs, hard-boiled
1 stalk lemongrass	1 large onion, cut into very thin rings
1 teaspoon salt	Vegetable oil
15 black peppercorns	1/3 cup peas, either fresh or frozen
1 pound samba or long-grain rice (2 2/3 cups)	3/4 cup salted cashew nuts
	3/4 cup sultanas, packed

METHOD

■ Melt the butter or ghee in a large saucepan over a low heat. Add the dry ingredients and rice, and stir until each grain of rice is coated.

■ Add the coconut milk, stock, and saffron in milk if using. Bring to a boil, then turn down the heat and simmer. Stir occasionally until the rice is cooked.

■ Meanwhile, prepare the garnish. Shell the hard-boiled eggs and cut each one into 4 (or 8 if large) segments. Fry the onion rings in a little oil until golden brown and set aside. Put the peas in a saucepan, cover them with water and bring to a boil for only a few seconds. Then plunge them into ice cold water and drain to keep them green and *al dente* ("with a bite," as the Italians say about spaghetti).

■ Remove as many whole spices from the rice as possible, turn out onto a large platter, and garnish with the hard-boiled eggs, onion rings, peas, cashew nuts, and sultanas.

Clockwise from top: Tiger Lily Sweet and Sour Sauce (page 26), toasted sesame seeds, Chicken Batons (page 107), Fried Seaweed (page 47), Onion Bhajiis (page 37), Mint and Yogurt Dip (page 39)

Clockwise from top: Satay Sauce (page 28), Gado Gado (page 144), Tiger Lily Tamarind Fish (page 120)

Clockwise from top: Seeni Sambol (page 33), Coconut Sambol (page 30), Sri Lankan Lamb and Spinach Curry (page 102), Yellow Rice (page 64)

Clockwise from top: Quick and Easy Naan Bread (page 80), Sambol Ulek (page 25), Lamb Kebobs in Coriander and Mint, with Lemon Yogurt (page 103)

Clockwise from top: Simple Malay Chicken Satay (page 94), served with Satay Sauce (page 28), Fried Rice Sticks with Seafood and Vegetables (page 88), Sri Lankan Hoppers (page 72), Pao (page 76), Stuffed Spring Rolls (page 48).

Clockwise from top: Indonesian Grilled Spicy Chicken (page 112), Stir-Fried Beans (page 149), Coconut Rotis (page 74).

Clockwise from top: Pineapple Curry (page 146), Tomato, Cucumber, & Onion Sambol (page 32), Channa (page 141), Roti Djala (page 75).

Top to bottom: Avocado Ice Cream (page 164) served on Sharp Fruit sauce (page 165), Almond Tea (page 158).

Milk Rice

SERVES 4 TO 6

At Sinhala (Sri Lankan) New Year, our cook would make *kiri bath* or milk rice. Part of the ritual would be to boil a small quantity of milk on the stove until it overflowed. This would guarantee good health and good fortune for the family. We always remember waking each Sinhala New Year's Day to the smell of burning milk accompanied by the loud bang of firecrackers. *Kiri bath* is also served for breakfast on the first day of each lunar month.

This recipe requires country rice, which is a lovely red color. It needs more liquid and a slightly longer cooking time than white long-grain rice.

INGREDIENTS

2 2/3 cups white or unmilled country rice	1 cup coconut milk
3 teaspoons salt	Butter to grease dish
3 1/4 cups water	

METHOD

■ Wash the rice, place in a saucepan with 3 1/4 cups water and the salt and bring to a boil.

■ Boil for about 10 to 15 minutes, then add the coconut milk.

■ Cover the pan with a tight-fitting lid, lower the heat, and simmer for 10 to 15 minutes.

■ Turn off the heat, but leave covered for another 5 minutes.

■ Butter a shallow flat dish, turn the rice into it and smooth the surface. Use a potato masher to mark the top of the rice in a pattern if desired.

■ Mark the rice into diamonds or squares with 2-inch sides and serve in the dish, with *Seeni Sambol* (page 33), Coconut Sambol (page 30), and Salt Fish Curry (page 122).

Chicken Rice

SERVES 4

Sidle up to a Malaysian or Singaporean and whisper "Chicken Rice" in their ear. They will adopt a yearning expression, their eyes will glaze over with remembered pleasure, and homesickness will definitely strike. If you visit this part of the world ask any taxi driver where you can get this dish. Everyone has their own favorite haunt.

Eating out here includes visiting the many hawker stands dotted by the roadside. People with gas cylinders and woks or metal trays will serve the freshest, most delicious food imaginable. There are food centers where you sit in the middle on tables and chairs. Around the sides will be stalls selling Chinese, Indian and Malaysian, or Thai specialties, cakes, desserts, and freshly made fruit juices. The cooks will come over to you, you choose what you want to eat and drink from the vast selection available, then pay at the end. We always order this dish.

Any leftover stock makes an ideal base for many of the soup and noodle recipes in this book. The meat from the chicken carcass is ideal for many of the stir-fry recipes, too.

INGREDIENTS

3 1/4-pound chicken (preferably free-range—corn-fed is very good)	2 teaspoons *tung choi* (preserved Chinese vegetable), optional
2 chicken stock cubes	4 slices fresh ginger
3 black peppercorns, crushed	1 1/3 cups long-grain rice
1/2 lemon, cut into slices	1 cucumber, cut into batons (see below)

METHOD

■ Put the chicken, breast-side down, in a deep pot with a lid; a pressure cooker is ideal.

■ Dissolve the stock cubes in 10 cups boiling water. Pour the stock over the chicken (it should just cover the bird), add all the ingredients except the rice and cucumber, bring to a boil, and cover. If you have the giblets, add them to the water to intensify the flavor. Boil for 10 minutes, turn the heat down, simmer for another 20 minutes, then turn the heat off. *Do not lift the lid off* but leave the chicken to cool for at least 4 hours. By that time it should be perfectly cooked, and not dry in the slightest.

■ Drain the chicken and cut the succulent meat into serving portions. Keep warm.

■ Fish out the ginger and lemon slices and discard. Save the stock.

■ Rinse the rice several times until the water runs clear. Leaving this stage out will mean healthier but less appetizing rice.

■ Put the rice in a pan with a tight-fitting lid. Add enough chicken stock to cover the rice, then enough extra stock to come 1 inch up the side of the pan. Bring the rice to a boil, then cover and simmer until perfectly cooked. Resist the urge to peek, so that the steam is retained in the pan.

■ Serve the chicken on a bed of rice with cucumber batons and some bottled chile sauce.

■ To make cucumber batons, wash the cucumber, hold it vertically and drag a fork down the sides, turning frequently to make ridges or stripes down the whole fruit. Cut the cucumber into 2-inch pieces, then into thick matchsticks.

VARIATION

If you are lucky enough to track down Szechuan peppercorns, crush 1 tablespoon sea salt and 1 tablespoon peppercorns together and serve in a small bowl. Guests take a pinch and sprinkle on their serving of Chicken Rice.

Biriyani

SAVORY RICE WITH MEAT

SERVES 6 TO 8

Grandfather, Francis Cooray, was a journalist, like our father, Dodwell. Dad has inherited much of his generosity of spirit and is one of life's true gentlemen, as well as being very modest. Now his greatest pleasure is having the family round for meals, and this is one of the special dishes that we always ask him to prepare for us.

INGREDIENTS

1 pound boned lamb or beef, chopped into 1-inch cubes	1/2 cup ghee
1 tablespoon rice wine vinegar	1 cup sliced onions
2 teaspoons ground coriander	3 garlic cloves, crushed
3 teaspoons ground cumin	2-inch piece of ginger, peeled and crushed
1 teaspoon ground turmeric	6 cardamom pods, lightly crushed
2 teaspoons salt	4 cloves
1 teaspoon ground black pepper	1 medium ripe tomato, chopped
5 1/3 cups Patna or samba rice	8 green chiles, chopped
	6 to 8 hard-boiled eggs, shelled

METHOD

■ Mix the meat with the vinegar, ground spices, salt, and pepper and set aside.

■ Wash the rice in running water and set aside.

■ Heat the ghee in a pan, add the onion, garlic, and ginger and fry until golden brown. Then add the cardamom pods, cloves, and meat. Keep stirring until all the liquid has evaporated and the meat begins to fry.

■ Add the rice, tomatoes, chiles and 8 cups water, bring to a boil, and cook for 10 to 15 minutes. Put on a tight-fitting lid, reduce the heat, and simmer until the rice is tender and the water has evaporated.

■ To serve, stir carefully so that the meat and vegetables are evenly distributed, turn onto a platter, and place the hard-boiled eggs in the rice so that each person has a generous helping of rice, meat, and a whole egg.

VARIATION

If desired, add Dry Potato and Coconut Curry (page 142) to the rice. Served with a few vegetable curries and sambols, this makes a substantial meal in itself and is ideal for entertaining.

Compressed Rice Cakes

SERVES 4 TO 6

These easy-to-prepare individual portions of rice are served with Thai, Malaysian, and Japanese dishes. They can be flavored by adding a number of different ingredients.

Make them the day before and store in the refrigerator. They can also be frozen on trays and defrosted a few at a time when needed. It's useful to keep an emergency supply for entertaining or when you fancy something different.

Use the same-sized cup to measure the rice and stock.

INGREDIENTS

2 cups short-grain rice	1 tablespoon grated fresh ginger *or* 5 kaffir lime leaves *or* the grated rind and juice of 2 lemons
4 cups chicken or vegetable stock (made with 2 stock cubes)	

METHOD

■ Do not wash the rice but place all the ingredients in a pan with a tight-fitting lid. Bring to a boil, lower the heat, and cook for about 30 minutes or until the rice is cooked and all the liquid has been absorbed.

■ Turn the rice into a well-oiled metal tray measuring about 6 x 10 inches, cover with 2 sheets of foil, and press down with a number of heavy weights—hardback books, cans, even full wine bottles! You want to compress the rice, so use quite heavy objects.

■ Leave overnight in the refrigerator.

■ Using a sharp knife, cut the rice into squares or diamond shapes. If the rice sticks, wet the blade in water. Turn out carefully and serve with curries or Simple Malay Beef Satay (page 94).

Chok

CHINESE WATERY RICE

SERVES 2 TO 3

Please do not shudder and quickly turn the page. Most Chinese eat *chok* for breakfast and, as there are several million of them, we reckon more people in the world sit down to this dish than cereal or porridge or even bacon and eggs. Although it may be a bit much, asking you to start the day off with this dish, it is quite delicious served as a light supper dish. It is good for convalescents as it is easily digested. Teamed up with Golden Coin Eggs (page 118), it was one of Rani's favorite childhood meals.

Mum would often decant the remnants of our refrigerator into *chok*, and then it became *bobo*—a very hit-and-miss family special. If we had curry, this went in, as well as any bits of stir-fries. It could be absolutely delicious and then again....We well remember a day when she was in more of a hurry than usual. *That* particular *bobo* had two ham sandwiches floating in it—not to be recommended! Finely shredded cooked meat, chicken, or fish are fine.

INGREDIENTS

1 1/4 cups cooked rice	2 teaspoons *tung choi* (preserved Chinese vegetable)
5 cups water or 2 1/4 cups Homemade Chicken Stock (page 29) or 2 good chicken or vegetable stock cubes dissolved in the same quantity of water	Ground white pepper (optional)
	Soy sauce (optional)
1 teaspoon salt	Scallions, washed, trimmed, and finely chopped

METHOD

■ Put the rice in a saucepan with all the ingredients, except the pepper, soy sauce, and scallions.

■ Bring to a boil, reduce the heat, cover, and simmer for about 30 minutes. The rice should have turned into something resembling very thin porridge.

■ Taste and adjust the seasoning. Add a little white ground pepper, extra salt or soy sauce if desired, sprinkle the chopped scallions on top, and serve.

BREADS AND PANCAKES

▲▲▲▲▲▲▲▲▲▲▲▲▲▲▲▲▲

Although we confess to loving rice more than anything else, we are rather fond of the recipes we share with you in this chapter. The flours we us are ordinary white or self-raising (white) flour, ground rice, or rice flour. All are freely available in supermarkets or local stores. Like whole-wheat flour, unmilled rice flour has a characteristic reddish color.

Back home the agent for *Thosais* and Hoppers would be toddy (fermented coconut water), which gives a slightly sour taste. However, through trial and error, we discovered that we got almost the same result in a much shorter time by using quick-rising yeast. If you are really impatient, do as we do and warm the flour before adding the yeast and liquid. A couple of minutes on low power in the microwave (taking care not to scorch or kill it) really gets that yeast going.

We also use yeast in our *Pao* (Chinese dumpling) recipe, although you will doubtless come across cooks who advocate using plain flour and boiling water. Ours come out fluffy and light; Mum, Dad, and the kids prefer them to the more traditional variety, which are rather heavy.

Everything in this chapter can be frozen if wrapped well, except for Hoppers. The craze for miniaturizing food (baby vegetables especially) is still going strong. We have been amused to see tiny individual portions of fish and chips wrapped in small sheets of newspaper, and tiny kebobs or bite-sized hamburgers appearing at some smart parties. We have often done the same with our *Naan* Bread and *Paos*.

Incidentally, for those travelers tempted by our stories to track down some genuine Sri Lankan toddy (our native hooch), please make sure you examine its origins very carefully. Without wishing to malign toddy-makers in general, we have seen all sorts of unsavory unwanted protein (dead insects and worse) floating in the buckets of less reputable manufacturers….

Sri Lankan Hoppers

MAKES 20 TO 24; ENOUGH FOR 6 TO 8

A hopper (or *appa*) is a crisp concave pancake with a spongy center. In Sri Lanka these bowl-shaped savories used to appear from breakfast until the early hours of the morning. Eaten with Coconut Sambol (page 30), curries, and lentils, or even jam and honey, they are one of the finest dishes we know. Many people have a balti pan (like a small wok) lurking in the back of the cupboard. They are perfect for making Hoppers, so drag them out, dust them off, and have a go. If you do not possess a balti pan, you can use the same mixture to make pancakes in a small frying pan. They will not look the same, although they will taste just as good.

Hoppers (and their lacy rice-flour cousins, Stringhoppers or strings, page 86) are the staple breakfast dish for most Sri Lankans. They were the specialty of the fisher folk who lived on the beach near our house, and we would order them the night before. They would arrive early in the morning, in a flat basket, covered with clean banana leaves still warm from the fire, with a small newspaper cone nestling underneath containing fiery Coconut Sambol. Delicious and costing just a few cents, they were the things we mourned most when we came to the West—just like we pined for Marmite, Walls bacon and sausages, and baked beans when we returned home!

Hoppers are best eaten fresh—tipped out of the pan onto someone's waiting plate—although you can keep them in an airtight container for the next day.

There is a definite skill to making these—judging how much oil to use to grease the pan, the consistency of the mixture, and how long to cook it. Like all pancakes, once you master the knack you will never forget it. If your first attempt fails, just throw it out, wipe the pan with oiled paper or cloth, and try again.

INGREDIENTS

1 3/4 cups rice (white or the unmilled red variety), ground	1 1/2 teaspoons sugar
	2 teaspoons salt
3 cups rice flour or plain white flour	1 teaspoon rice wine vinegar
3/4 cup coconut milk	Oil, to grease frying pan
1 packet quick-rising dried yeast	

METHOD

■ Mix all the ingredients, except the oil, in a deep bowl, together with 6 cups hand-hot water, and leave in a warm place until thick and frothy and doubled in size. Sri Lankans start it off the night before, if Hoppers are on the menu for breakfast. The batter should be the consistency of cream, but thin enough to form a transparent skin up the sides of the pan. Only trial and error will give you the right consistency, and every batch will be different according to the flour uses (or even the weather!).

■ Brush a balti pan or deep frying pan with oil and heat on a gas or electric ring. When the oil smokes, pour in a tablespoonful of batter. Using a thick cloth, pick up the pan with both hands and roll it until the sides are coated about two-thirds of the way up.

■ Cover with a tight-fitting lid or ovenproof plate and cook over a very low heat for 5 minutes or until the sides are brown and the center is set.

■ Use a metal spatula to gently ease the hopper from the sides of the pan and slip it out onto a plate. Oil the pan and continue until all the mixture is used up.

■ Hoppers should be crisp on the outside and soft and spongy in the middle.

VARIATION

To make an **egg hopper,** break an egg into the uncooked hopper at the end of step 2 of the above recipe. Cover and cook over a low heat, as described above, until the egg is set.

Coconut Rotis

MAKES 16;
ENOUGH FOR
6 TO 8

This round flat bread or pancake flavored with coconut is very simple to make but deliciously different. When we were not gorging on hoppers or strings it made a good breakfast alternative. After lessons had ended at the Methodist College for Girls, Colombo, in the early afternoon, we would go over to Aunty Lulu's in Colpetty and wait for Dad to pick us up after work. Aunty Lulu's cook and *amah* made the most delicious afternoon tiffin, or snacks. Although we were both very chubby, we would try very hard to suck in our cheeks and look like starving waifs. This trick usually worked and nearly every day we were invited by our soft-hearted cousins, Sonia and Aloma, to join them for tea. Their *amah* made the best *rotis* in the world.

Rotis will freeze but are best eaten hot and fresh.

INGREDIENTS

4 cups self-rising wheat flour or rice flour (use 1 teaspoon baking powder sifted with the rice flour)	1 small green chile, chopped
	4 curry leaves, crumbled (optional)
1 1/2 cups dried coconut (fine cut)	1 egg, whisked
1 teaspoon salt	1 tablespoon oil, to grease frying pan

METHOD

■ Mix all the dry ingredients in a bowl, add the egg, then add about 1 cup water, a little at a time, to form a stiff dough.

■ Knead for a few moments on a floured surface, then put the dough into an oiled bag (see *Pao* recipe, step 3, page 76) and leave in a warm place for about 45 minutes.

■ Divide the dough into 16 equal balls, then roll each into a circle about the size of a saucer, on a floured surface.

■ Lightly grease a heavy frying pan and cook over a medium heat for about 4 minutes. Turn over and cook on the other side.

VARIATION

If desired, add 1/2 teaspoon grated maldive fish to the mixture before adding the water.

Roti Djala

LACY INDONESIAN PANCAKES

SERVES 4 TO 6

These delicate filigree circles echo the ornate molding found in Oriental temples. They are traditionally made by dipping the fingers of one hand in the batter, then letting it fall in four steady strings. But a satisfactory effect can be gained by using a small teaspoon and pouring a steady thin stream of batter in random patterns across a hot frying pan.

In Sri Lanka we would use a small tuft of coconut husk (*copra*) dipped in oil to grease a pan or hopper mold. Now we make do with a piece of paper towel or a clean rag.

These pancakes are served with dry curries and sambols.

INGREDIENTS

1 3/4 cups coconut milk	1/2 teaspoon salt
2 cups white flour	Oil, to grease frying pan
2 eggs, beaten	

METHOD

■ Use a blender or whisk to mix all the ingredients, except the oil, into a smooth lump-free batter.

■ Heat a lightly greased frying pan. When it starts to smoke, dip your fingers (or a teaspoon) into the batter and move across the pan to resemble a lace pattern. Do not make it too full of holes or you will have difficulty scooping up your curry with the completed pancake!

■ Turn the pancake over and cook for a couple of seconds until it begins to brown at the edges. Repeat until all the batter is used up. The batter may be thicker as you come to the bottom of the bowl. If so, just add a little water to thin it down.

Pao

STUFFED STEAMED CHINESE DUMPLINGS

**MAKES 12;
ENOUGH
FOR 6**

There are four main regions in China, the cuisine of each reflecting its climate and harvest. Beijing (Peking) cuisine dominates the northern region. This area specializes in locally grown wheat products such as pancakes, buns (*pao*), and *zchotse*, a soft deep-fried bread stick like a salty doughnut. Meats are served with rich sweet-and-sour sauces and dips based on red beans. The best-known dish from this area is, of course, Peking Duck.

Pao are steamed stuffed bread dumplings that can be made in different sizes. We favor smaller ones, about 1 1/2 inches in diameter. Two of these, served with a selection of chile and sweet-and-sour sauces, make a delicious starter. Make a double quantity and freeze in individual plastic bags. When you fancy a late-night TV snack, just defrost and enjoy them with a choice of sauces and chile dips.

INGREDIENTS

6 tablespoons milk	1 teaspoon sugar
2 cups self-raising flour	1/4 teaspoon salt
1/2 packet quick-rising dried yeast	Oil

METHOD

■ Mix the milk with 6 tablespoons boiling water in a large bowl. Add the rest of the ingredients and mix to a soft dough.

■ Turn out onto a floured surface. Knead until the ball of dough becomes smooth and elastic.

■ Put the dough into a large oiled plastic bag. To oil the bag, place 1 teaspoon oil inside it and rub together until all the inside surfaces are covered. Tie a knot at the top giving the dough plenty of room to rise. Leave to double in size in a warm place. You will find this method is quick and simple—try it for proving traditional yeast-based Western dough recipes, too.

■ Prepare the filling (see opposite, and page 78) and put aside to cool.

■ When the dough is spongy and light, open the bag and tip onto a floured surface. Divide into 12 balls.

■ Pat each ball out to a circle about the size of your palm. Put 1 1/2 teaspoons filling in the middle, then gather the edges together and pinch to seal.

- Turn the balls over, taking care not to let any of the filling escape.

- Cut a circle of greaseproof paper the size of your steamer and line the top half. Place the dumplings on the paper-lined half, leaving plenty of space between them as they will double in size.

- Steam over rapidly boiling water for 10 to 15 minutes, until the dumplings are light, fluffy, and cooked.

Stir-Fried Filling

INGREDIENTS

8 ounces any left-over stir-fired vegetable or meat mixture (about 2 cups)	1 teaspoon cornstarch (optional)
	1/2 teaspoon sherry (optional)

METHOD

- If very watery, thicken the stir-fried filling with the cornstarch mixed with the sherry and 1 tablespoon water.

- Add to the filling and boil until thickened.

Pork Filling

INGREDIENTS

1 teaspoon oil	1 teaspoon cornstarch
1 cup sliced Char Sui Pork (page 98)	1/2 teaspoon sherry
1/3 cup bamboo shoots	1 teaspoon soy sauce
1/2 cup bean sprouts	

METHOD

- Heat the oil in a frying pan. Add the pork, bamboo shoots, and bean sprouts and stir-fry for 2 minutes.

- Mix the cornstarch with the sherry, soy sauce, and 1 tablespoon water.

- Add to the filling and boil until thickened.

Chicken Filling

INGREDIENTS

1 tablespoon sliced onion	1 teaspoon cornstarch
1 cup sliced chicken breast (cooked or raw)	1/2 teaspoon sherry
1/2 teaspoon oil	1 tablespoon soy sauce
1/2 teaspoon sugar	1/8 to 1/2 teaspoon grated fresh ginger

METHOD

■ Fry the onion and chicken in the oil.

■ Mix the sugar and cornstarch with the sherry, soy sauce, and 1 tablespoon water. Add to the filling, with the ginger, and boil until thickened.

Thosais

MALAYSIAN SAVORY PANCAKES

**MAKES 24;
SERVES 6**

One of our kids' favorite uncles is Desmond, the retired general manager of Kuala Lumpur airport. They love him because he is always full of tricks and jokes (usually naughty ones). His wife, saintly Aunty Daisy, can only remonstrate with a gentle "Must you, Desmond?" and he generally does!

When we stayed with Uncle Desmond, he insisted on trying to get us to eat every Malaysian specialty known to man. Ignoring our weak protests, he would push us out of bed at 5:30 AM and drag us off to eat freshly made *thosais*.

Thosais are very popular in South India and Sri Lanka as well as Malaysia. As with all flour-based recipes, it is difficult to give the exact amount of water needed for these savory pancakes. Add more plain flour to the mixture if the batter seems too thin, or a little water if it is too thick. It should be like thick cream.

INGREDIENTS

1 1/2 cups *urid dhal* (ask for these small black lentils at your local Asian or health food store)

1/2 quantity Hopper mixture (page 72)

2 teaspoons oil

1/2 teaspoon mustard seeds

2 curry leaves, crumbled (optional)

1/2 small onion, very finely chopped

2 to 3 teaspoons salt to taste

1 small green chile, finely chopped

Oil, to grease the frying pan

METHOD

■ Soak the lentils overnight in at least 2 quarts water. Next day, rinse well in fresh running water, then grind in a blender with 2/3 cup water. Add some of the hopper mixture if needed. This mixture should be a smooth lump-free paste.

■ Stir in the remaining hopper mixture and set aside.

■ Heat the oil in a frying pan, add the mustard seeds and curry leaves if used, and fry until the seeds pop. Add the chopped onion and fry until golden.

■ Mix the batter with the cooled onion mixture, salt, and chile, and stir well. Brush the base of a heavy frying pan with a little oil and spread 2 tablespoons batter over the pan with a metal spatula or the blade of a knife. Turn once, then cook on the other side.

■ Repeat until all the batter is used up, oiling the pan between each thosai. Eat freshly made with a selection of curries.

Quick and Easy Naan Bread

MAKES 6

Light fluffy *naans*, ready to be enhanced with your own toppings…Although some supermarkets stock this gorgeous bread, this recipe really is easy, so do try it.

Rani now lives in Walthamstow, England, close to an amazing tandoori takeaway. Run by an elderly husband and wife from their converted front room, it is unbelievably cheap. Customers are treated to a real double act as they argue over orders. Everything is freshly cooked, and they bring out teaspoons for customers to taste and adjust the seasonings while their food is prepared. Fast food it is not!

Although their kitchen is small, it is immaculately clean and a huge electric tandoor oven takes pride of place. Made from a special stone, the inside resembles an Ali Baba basket. The wife rolls out the dough for the *naan*, then leans in and slaps the bread directly onto the heated walls of the tandoor. It hangs there, defying gravity, and after about 2 minutes she turns it with a long fork and bakes the other side. Almost instantly it puffs up in the scorching heat, and brown spots cover the surface.

The following method tries to simulate the tandoor. Make sure your oven is red hot before you put the trays in. You will need a separate oven and broiler.

INGREDIENTS

4 cups self-rising flour and 1/2 teaspoon baking powder, sifted together	2 eggs
1/2 teaspoon salt	3 tablespoons melted butter, to glaze
2 tablespoons oil	2 tablespoons black poppy or sesame seeds (optional)
4 tablespoons plain yogurt	

METHOD

■ Mix all the ingredients, except the melted butter and poppy or sesame seeds, in a large bowl.

■ Add 1/2 to 2/3 cup water, a little at a time, kneading well between additions, to form a soft dough.

■ Put into an oiled bag (see Pao recipe, step 3, page 76) and leave to rest for 30 minutes.

■ Preheat the oven to its highest temperature and place 2 heavy metal baking trays upside down in the oven to heat up. At the same time, put the broiler on its highest setting.

■ Divide the dough into 6 equal balls. Roll out on a floured surface into either a round or the more traditional tear shape.

■ Carefully take out the hot trays with oven mitts, slap 1 to 2 *naans* (depending on the size of your *naan* and tray) onto them and bake for about 3 minutes.

■ Remove from the oven and flash broil for 30 seconds to 1 minute.

■ Brush the top with melted butter, and if desired, sprinkle with either poppy or sesame seeds.

■ Remove the *naan* from the tray, put it back in the oven to reheat, remove the other tray and repeat the process. With a little practice, you can get a production line of trays going in and out of the oven. The trays will be very hot so watch out for accidents when drafting in any helpers.

VARIATIONS

■ Thinly slice 2 onions and fry in 2 teaspoons oil until just softened. At step 6, press the fried onions onto the top of the *naan* before baking, to make a sort of Asian pizza.

■ Microwave or boil a medium-sized potato until half-cooked. Dice, and sauté in 1 teaspoon oil until just turning brown. Press into the *naan* dough at step 6, then sprinkle with a little sea salt, ground red pepper, and 1 teaspoon finely chopped coriander (cilantro) leaves before baking.

Peking Pancakes or Spring Roll Wrappers

MAKES 36; ENOUGH FOR 6 TO 8 AS MAIN MEAL (OR, IF ROLLED OUT SMALLER, MAKES 50 MINI-WRAPPERS FOR A BUFFET)

Coming from the fierce north of China, Mother grew up on *pao* and other wheat products, as well as the pancakes that accompany Peking duck. She tells of meals where small bamboo steamers with these pancakes in them would be brought to the table and guests and family would help themselves to a variety of fillings, roll the pancakes up, and eat them with a dipping sauce.

The pancakes can be made the day before. Cover with plastic wrap or foil so they do not dry out, and steam when ready to serve. If you want to serve these as Mother describes, we suggest you team them up with roast duck, Char Sui Pork (page 98), cucumber batons (page 67), shredded scallions, lightly steamed Chinese cabbage, bean sprouts, and mushrooms. Good sauces would be hoisin or Quick Plum Sauce (page 27), *Sambol Ulek* (page 25), and Satay Sauce (page 28). Or eat them with Vietnamese Dipping Sauce (page 25).

By sheer necessity (big party to cater for and not enough wrappers), we discovered that these pancakes made good spring roll wrappers, too.

INGREDIENTS

4 cups white flour	1 teaspoon sesame oil
1/2 teaspoon salt	Extra flour, to roll out pancakes

METHOD

- Sift the flour and salt into a large bowl.

- Combine about 1 cup boiling water with the sesame oil, pour into the flour and mix to a soft dough.

- Knead for 5 to 10 minutes on a floured surface until the dough becomes smooth. Cover and leave for 30 minutes.

- Divide the dough into 36 or 50 equal-sized balls. Then roll each out on a floured surface until it is very thin (you should be about to see through them).

- Heat a nonstick frying pan, then dry-fry the pancakes for a few seconds on either side. They will develop small brown spots when they are done.

- Put in a steamer and steam for 10 minutes before serving.

NOODLES

▲▲▲▲▲▲▲▲▲▲▲▲▲▲▲▲▲

Oodles and oodles of wonderful noodles! Noodles come in all shapes and sizes, from the ubiquitous yellow egg noodles to the more unfamiliar white rice noodles. The Chinese claim that the Italians learned how to eat pasta from Marco Polo— once they had introduced him to this most popular food!

Some noodles are very thick (the better to soak up rich sauces) and others almost hair-thin. Rice sticks (*meehoon*) are a staple found all across Southeast Asia. They are eaten in soup, deep-fried until crispy and served with a sauce, or stir-fried with almost every imaginable combination of ingredients.

A very unusual noodle is the cellophane, thread, or bean vermicelli, made from mung beans. Fine and light when dry, it becomes slippery and transparent when boiled in hot soups or sauces. It is nourishing and easily digested and Thais often use it as an ingredient in their spring roll fillings. We advise you to cut it into manageable lengths before cooking, as it is impossible to do so when cooked.

When we were small, we were embarrassed by the way our Chinese and Malaysian friends ate noodles and rice. A small bowl would be held close to the mouth and the noodles sucked up very noisily with a loud slurp. Rice would be shoveled in with a pair of chopsticks held close together. This was when our different backgrounds began to grate against each other. Though a mortal offense in Western society, eating this way is seen as good form in the East in the same way as a loud belch at the end of a meal and a dirty tablecloth are considered compliments to the cook.

As we began to travel more extensively we became older, wiser, and more tolerant, and can now slurp with the best of them!

Lo Mein

LONG-LIFE NOODLES WITH BEEF & VEGETABLES

SERVES 4 TO 6

A Manchurian by birth, our Chinese *Kung Kung* (grandfather) brought his family to live within the gates of the Forbidden City in Peking. The family's diet was based on flour products and not rice. We well remember Chinese New Year and January 1st. Mum would prepare a large dish of long-life noodles, partly to remember *Kung Kung* by, but also to ensure that we all lived long and healthy lives.

INGREDIENTS

Pinch of salt	4 scallions, washed, trimmed, and chopped, or 2 onions, thinly sliced
8 ounces dried egg noodles	
1 pound beef steak, cut into very thin strips	1 cup sliced bamboo shoots
	1 green chile, chopped (optional)
3 tablespoons soy sauce	2 teaspoons sugar
2 teaspoons cornstarch	1 tablespoon hoisin sauce
2 tablespoons oil	1/4 cup bean sprouts

METHOD

▪ Put 2 quarts water in a large saucepan over a high heat. Add a pinch of salt and, when boiling, drop in the egg noodles. Cook for 8 to 10 minutes, or according to the directions on the packet. Drain and set aside.

▪ Toss the meat in 1 tablespoon soy sauce mixed with the cornstarch. Set aside.

▪ Heat the oil in a wok and, when smoking, stir-fry the scallions and then the beef. Cook, stirring continuously, until the beef changes color.

▪ Add the bamboo shoots, chile if using, sugar, hoisin sauce, the rest of the soy sauce, and the bean sprouts. Stir-fry for 1 minute.

▪ Lastly, add the noodles and toss so that all the ingredients are well mixed.

VARIATION

This makes a very good vegetarian dish. Omit the beef and substitute 1 cup each of carrot sticks, shredded *pak choi* (Chinese cabbage), mushrooms, and 1/2 teaspoon *Sambol Ulek* (page 25).

Easiest Mixed Fried Noodles Ever

SERVES 4 TO 6

If you live within walking distance of a supermarket with a deli counter you could be eating this in 5 minutes—really!

INGREDIENTS

8 ounces 3-minute (ramen) egg noodles or ordinary spaghetti	1 garlic clove, crushed
Salt	1 large onion, finely sliced
4 ounces cooked ham	1/2 cup water chestnuts, cut into quarters
4 ounces sliced chicken breast	1 cup bean sprouts
4 ounces roast beef	2 teaspoons Thai Red Curry Paste 1 or 2 (page 20)
1 tablespoon oil	

METHOD

■ Boil the noodles or spaghetti according to the directions on the packet in plenty of salted boiling water. Drain and keep warm.

■ Meanwhile cut the sliced meats into thin strips and set aside.

■ Put the oil into a preheated wok, heat, and add the garlic and onion. Stir-fry to 2 minutes.

■ Add the water chestnuts, bean sprouts, and meat and warm through for a few moments. Add the noodles and curry paste. Check the seasoning, adding a pinch of salt if necessary.

■ Serve on a large tray and dig in!

VARIATION

The discerning cook will seize on this recipe as a way of using up leftover roasts and quite rightly so! To give it a new twist, add a splash of ginger wine or sherry.

Mock Stringhoppers

SERVES 6

Some of our best times in Sri Lanka were the regular weekend dances at the Otters' Swimming Club (where we would bump into life member Arthur C. Clarke) or at the Dutch Burgher Union. Listening to a live band, complete with groovy saxophone, meeting our schoolfriends and relations of all ages, dancing under the stars, the air full of flickering fireflies and chirping crickets were our pleasures for the evening—and then there was the drive home: stopping on the way at some roadside *kade* (eating shack) where someone would be steaming crisp stringhoppers over an open fire and serving them with searingly hot curries.

Unless you have a village *kade*, or someone prepared to spend about three hours in the kitchen roasting rice flour, sifting it, making the paste, squeezing it out through a mold in strings onto individual mats and steaming it (oh really!), it's much better to try our mock stringhoppers.

"Strings" are a much-loved dish in Sri Lanka, and can be eaten for breakfast, lunch, or dinner.

INGREDIENTS

**1-pound packet Chinese rice sticks
(*meehoon*)**

Salt

METHOD

■ Bring a very large pan of salted water to a boil, drop in the rice sticks, and stir to separate.

■ Boil for only 2 minutes, then immediately strain off the water. Put the rice sticks in an ovenproof dish and place in a steamer.

■ Steam for 5 minutes and serve with *Hodi* (page 55), omelet, Coconut Sambol (page 30), *Seeni Sambol* (page 33), *Mallung* (page 140), and any curries you wish.

Transparent Noodles with Mushrooms & Pork or Shrimp

SERVES 3 TO 4

Cellophane Noodles are also called transparent noodles. They are very easy to digest and slippery to eat. Because they are so light it is difficult to weigh them. Try making a ring out of your thumb and index finger and gather a bunch of noodles about that diameter for this recipe. Use a pair of scissors to cut the dry noodles into manageable pieces.

INGREDIENTS

2 ounces transparent noodles	1/2 teaspoon *Sambol Ulek* (page 25) or Tabasco sauce
4 tablespoons oil	2 tablespoons soy sauce
4 scallions, washed, trimmed, and chopped	1 tablespoon sherry
8 ounces ground pork, or 8 ounces fresh good-quality shrimp, shelled and roughly chopped	Grated rind of 1 lemon
	Salt
1 1/2 cups sliced button mushrooms	Pinch of five-spice powder

METHOD

■ Soak the noodles in plenty of lukewarm water for 30 minutes, drain, and set aside.

■ Heat the oil in a wok, then stir-fry the scallions, pork or shrimp, and mushrooms for 3 minutes.

■ Add the noodles and the rest of the ingredients, except the salt and five-spice powder, and boil until the liquid has evaporated.

■ Pile onto a warmed dish, season to taste with salt, sprinkle with the five-spice powder, and serve with rice.

Fried Rice Sticks with Seafood & Vegetables

SERVES 4 TO 6

The easiest meals can be prepared by using economical *meehoon* or rice sticks. These noodles need no cooking—just soak for about 30 minutes in warm water, drain, and they are ready to be stir-fried with any of the meat or vegetable recipes in this book.

Meehoon is an ideal standby when catering for unexpected visitors. Bundles of the white string-like noodles are readily available, tied into four portions with ribbon or string. A 1-pound pack will feed four to six people comfortably.

Other vegetables, such as red and yellow peppers and zucchini, can be added or substituted for any of the vegetables given below. For the seafood, try to include peeled shrimp, clams, or squid.

INGREDIENTS

1 large carrot, peeled	1 tablespoon soy sauce
1 1/2 cups button mushrooms, wiped	3 tablespoons chicken stock or water
2 leeks or onions, trimmed	4 ounces seafood (any variety or a mixture of several types)
3 tablespoons oil	
1 garlic clove, crushed	2 tablespoons sherry
4 bacon slices, cut into thin strips	1/2 teaspoon *Sambol Ulek* (page 25, optional)
1 1/2 cups finely shredded green cabbage	
1 teaspoon salt	1-pound package rice sticks (*meehoon*), soaked and drained (see above)
1/2 teaspoon white pepper	1/2 teaspoon sesame oil (optional)

METHOD

■ Cut the carrot, mushrooms, and leeks or onions into matchsticks, approximately 1 inch in length.

■ Heat the oil in a wok and stir-fry the onions or leeks and garlic for 2 minutes. Add the bacon, carrot sticks, and cabbage and fry for 2 minutes more.

■ Add all the rest of the ingredients, except the noodles and sesame oil. Mix well.

■ Finally add the noodles and fry for about 3 minutes or until most of the liquid has been absorbed by the noodles.

■ Mix in the sesame oil, if using, and serve.

VARIATION

Beat 2 eggs with 1 tablespoon water and 1/2 teaspoon salt. Use 2 tablespoons at once in a nonstick frying pan to make 2 very thin omelets. Turn over and, when cooked, stack on a plate. Repeat until all the egg mixture has been used up. Roll each omelet into a cigar shape, cut into thin shreds, and use to garnish the *meehoon*.

Fried Crispy Rice Sticks

SERVES 4

This Thai specialty is a very easy-to-make all-in-one dish for family and friends.

INGREDIENTS

2 1/4 cups oil for deep-frying	4 ounces fresh shrimp
8 ounces rice sticks (*meehoon*)	3 1/2 cups bean sprouts
1 onion, finely chopped	1 bunch or about 6 large scallions, washed, trimmed, and chopped
2 garlic cloves, finely chopped	
4 ounces pork tenderloin, sliced into thin strips	1 tablespoon lemon juice
	1 tablespoon soy sauce
4 ounces boneless, skinless chicken breast, sliced into thin strips	2 tablespoons fish sauce
	2 tablespoons rice wine vinegar

METHOD

■ Heat the oil in a wok. When very hot, put small handfuls of rice sticks in and fry until crisp. Remove with a metal spatula and drain on paper towels. Fry all the noodles this way.

■ Carefully pour all but 4 tablespoons of the oil into a metal container and use for some other purpose.

■ Put the wok back on the heat, and stir-fry the onion and garlic in the 4 tablespoons of oil until golden brown. Add the pork, chicken, and shrimp and cook until the flesh just turns opaque (about 3 minutes).

■ Add all the remaining ingredients except the deep-fried noodles. Mix well.

■ Finally, toss in the noodles, stir, and serve.

VARIATION

Garnish with chopped coriander (cilantro) leaves and a sprinkling of *Balichaw* (page 23).

Laksa

MALAYSIAN CURRIED SOUP

SERVES 4 TO 6

This savory spicy noodle dish is full of fish, shrimp, and seafood in a coconut sauce and is a national dish. We have amended it slightly but all the flavors echo *laksa* as we remember it. *Laksa* is a cross between a soup and a noodle dish. A bowlful makes a satisfying main course.

INGREDIENTS

8 ounces rice vermicelli	1 3/4 cups bean sprouts
1/2 teaspoon salt	4 scallions, washed, trimmed, and chopped
1/2 teaspoon ground black pepper	1 whole cucumber, finely sliced
8 ounces boneless white fish fillets, skinned	1 teaspoon shrimp paste (*blachan*), mixed to a paste with 1 teaspoon water
2 tablespoons flour, to roll fish balls	1/4 cup coconut milk
2/3 cup fresh or canned crabmeat	1 teaspoon oil
8 ounces peeled shrimp	2 kaffir lime leaves (optional)

METHOD

■ Soak the vermicelli in boiling water for 10 minutes, drain, and set aside.

■ Put the salt, pepper, and fish into a blender or food processor and process until it forms a paste. Flour your hands and shape the paste into 1-inch balls.

■ Bring 4 cups water to a boil in a pan, carefully lower the fish balls into it, and simmer for 2 minutes. Remove with a slotted spoon.

■ Add all the remaining ingredients to the water in the pan and bring to a boil. Stir carefully to mix the flavors, then simmer for 3 to 4 minutes.

■ Return the fish balls to the soup and serve in deep bowls with lime wedges and a small dish of *Sambol Ulek* (page 25).

VARIATION

We have made our own *laksa* with plain boiled spaghetti, leftover beef, lamb or chicken curry, and extra water. As long as the bean sprouts and cucumber are included, and the dish is spiced with coconut milk and *blachan* and served with lime wedges, it makes a tolerable substitute and is a great way to use up leftovers.

91

Spicy Noodles with Barbecued Meat & Spinach

SERVES 4 TO 6

A wonderful way of using up any leftover Char Sui Pork (page 98) or Satay (page 94) meat, this supper dish is quick and easy to prepare and best served freshly made.

INGREDIENTS

1 pound egg noodles	1/2 teaspoon ground cumin
2 tablespoons oil	1/2 teaspoon salt
1 garlic clove, crushed	1 small red chile, chopped
2 cups cooked cubed meat	1 tablespoon soy sauce
8 ounces spinach, washed and cut into strips	1 tablespoon cornstarch, mixed with 2 tablespoons sherry
1/2 teaspoon ground coriander	

METHOD

■ Cook the noodles in plenty of boiling water. Drain and keep to one side.

■ Heat the oil in a wok and, when smoking, add the garlic. Stir-fry for a few seconds, then add the meat, spinach, coriander, cumin, and salt. Stir-fry for 2 minutes.

■ Add the noodles, chile, and soy sauce, and then the cornstarch mixture.

■ Stir constantly until the sauce thickens.

VARIATIONS

■ If you prefer a hotter dish, add 1/2 to 1 teaspoon *Sambol Ulek* (page 25).

■ We sometimes stir in 2 teaspoons crunchy peanut butter to give a subtle nutty undertone and a more Indonesian flavor. Cream the peanut butter with the cornstarch and sherry mixture and add at step 3.

MEAT

▲▲▲▲▲▲▲▲▲▲▲▲▲▲▲▲

Unlike most Westerners, Asian people tend to eat only very small amounts of protein. Instead, we enjoy many different types of dishes—rice, flour products, vegetables, seafood or fish, and meat—at one meal.

The eating patterns of this part of the world largely reflect the many different religions found here: the Christians and Chinese have few taboos and eat practically anything, Muslims will not eat pork, and Hindus abhor beef.

Cooking styles also vary—from braising or stewing (curries and Chinese red cooking in soy sauce rely on these methods) to very quick stir-frying, grilling, and barbecuing. The cooking style is partly determined by the cut of meat—expensive tender cuts, such as frying steak, or fillet of lamb or pork, are ideal for fast cooking. By contrast, meat from parts of the animal which have to work harder (including the legs, haunches, and neck) are muscular and need slow cooking to tenderize the flesh. These are the cheaper cuts, marked stewing or braising meat.

Most of our recipes can be adapted to use any other protein, whether meat or fish.

One ingredient common to curries all over this region is a small quantity (about a teaspoon) of either dried salted shrimp or maldive fish. Believe us, the fishy taste is not apparent, but the curries have a note or depth when cooked this way that is most pleasant, and so unlike the curries you may be used to eating.

Simple Malay Beef Satay

SERVES 6

Dad lived in Malaysia for the first 30–odd years of his life, and it was here that he met and wooed our mother, Koh Yue Woon, whose stage name was Anna Koh. Not surprisingly, the cuisines of Malaysia and Singapore are very important to our family. We naturally gravitate to the Asian/Chinese sweet/hot/sour/spicy flavors of this region. Satay—small chunks of meat soaked in a spicy marinade and then grilled, broiled, or barbecued on sticks—is definitely one of our favorites. Satay means "three" in a Malaysian dialect—traditionally only three pieces of meat were skewered on each stick.

INGREDIENTS

1 1/2 pounds good-quality steak	1 1/2 teaspoon salt
1 tablespoon jaggery (palm sugar) or dark brown sugar	1 teaspoon ground red pepper
2 teaspoons ground turmeric	1 teaspoon lime or lemon juice
2 teaspoons ground cumin	1/4 cup coconut milk
2 teaspoons ground coriander	50 bamboo skewers, soaked in water

METHOD

■ Cut the beef into 1/2-inch cubes.

■ Mix all the ingredients in a large bowl, add the beef, and marinate for at least 2 hours. Overnight is best.

■ Thread the beef cubes onto skewers.

■ Preheat the grill to high and cook the meat, basting with leftover marinade and turning the sticks frequently. The sticks are done when the beef is brown and the delicious smells make your guests start chewing the carpet in anticipation.

■ Serve with Compressed Rice Cakes (page 69), Satay Sauce (page 28), and chile sauce. We serve fresh salads as well, and a bowl of cucumber batons (page 67).

VARIATION

Chicken satay is very good, too. Use breast meat cut into long strips and thread each strip onto a skewer. Brush with oil before grilling.

Beef Smoore

—— SRI LANKAN BRAISED BEEF IN A SPICY COCONUT SAUCE ——

**SERVES 6 TO 8
AS A MAIN
DISH, OR 15
AS PART OF A
BUFFET**

We really love this dish—the gravy is rich and savory, redolent of spices and coconut milk. *Smoore* makes an unusual buffet dish that benefits from being made a few days in advance. We usually make it at Christmas when palates are jaded by the everlasting turkey—Boxing Day is certainly enlivened by this recipe. Cut the meat into very thin pieces and serve with boiled rice, salads, and *Seeni Sambol* (page 33).

Try to get stewing beef, which has a fringe of fat, and is marbled with it, too. The fat keeps the meat from drying out and makes for succulent eating.

INGREDIENTS

3-pound piece of stewing beef or pot roast	2 teaspoons ground turmeric
2 medium onions, chopped	1 tablespoon ground cumin
5 cloves garlic, crushed	2 teaspoons ground mixed spices or allspice
1 tablespoon chopped fresh ginger	2 teaspoons salt
1 stick of cinnamon	2 teaspoons freshly ground black pepper
2 cloves	1/2 cup tamarind, pulp dissolved in hot water, *or* the juice of 3 lemons and 1 teaspoon brown sugar
2 star anise	
12 curry leaves (optional)	
1 stalk lemongrass (or the grated rind of 1 lemon)	1/2 teaspoon fenugreek seeds (optional)
3 tablespoons rice wine vinegar	1 cup coconut milk
1 tablespoon ground red pepper	3 tablespoons ghee or coconut oil

METHOD

■ Use a long metal skewer and stab the meat all over, very deeply. This is very therapeutic in the stressful days during the run up to Christmas!

■ Put all the ingredients, except the coconut milk and ghee or oil, in a pan and cook over a medium heat, covered, for 1 to 1 1/2 hours, or until the meat is tender, but not falling apart. Add extra water, if needed, to keep it from sticking to the bottom of the pan.

■ Add the coconut milk and cook, uncovered, over a high heat for another 10 minutes, or until most of the liquid has reduced. Keep turning the meat and stirring the bottom so the sauce does not catch. It should be the consistency of thick jam. Pick out and discard the largest pieces of spices.

■ Remove the meat. Put the oil in a wok and heat. When smoking, carefully put the meat in (be careful of splattering fat) and fry on all sides until a rich brown. Add the sauce and heat through.

VARIATION

Boneless lamb and pork roasts are equally good for this dish. Select cuts marbled with fat to keep the meat moist.

Beef Rendang

SERVES 4 TO 6 **R**endang is a hot, spicy, and dry dish and variations on it pop up in Indonesia, Malaysia, Singapore, and Bali. *Rendang* can be kept in the refrigerator for up to four days. The flavors develop and mature, so it is ideal for parties when you want to prepare as much in advance as possible. Serve with freshly boiled rice, Gado Gado (page 144), and Satay Sauce (page 28).

INGREDIENTS

1 tablespoon ground coriander	1 tablespoon tamarind juice (1 tablespoon tamarind pulp mixed with 3 tablespoons hot water, then strained)
1 tablespoon ground cumin	
1 teaspoon salt	1 large onion, cut into chunks
1 teaspoon turmeric	3 garlic cloves, crushed
1 teaspoon ground red pepper	1 teaspoon peeled and crushed ginger
2 teaspoons jaggery (palm sugar) or dark brown sugar	3 cardamom pods, crushed
1/2 cup coconut milk	1 stalk lemongrass, cut into small pieces
1/4 teaspoon ground black pepper	1 tablespoon oil
	1 pound good-quality steak, cut into thin strips

METHOD

■ Put all the ingredients, except the oil and meat, into a blender with 1 cup water, and blend to an almost smooth liquid paste.

■ Heat the oil in a pan and brown the meat strips. Add the prepared paste and bring to a boil.

■ Reduce the heat and cook until all the water has evaporated and the meat begins to fry. Keep stirring to prevent the meat catching and burning.

VARIATION

Lamb and pork are also good made into *rendang*. Choose tender cuts.

Char Sui Pork

ROAST OR BARBECUED CHINESE PORK

SERVES 4 AS
A MAIN MEAL,
OR 8 AS PART
OF A BUFFET

A classic, this is a very easy-to-make, but beautiful, dish, with its dark outside rim surrounding a pale juicy center. Char Sui pork or lamb fillet is delicious cooked on the barbecue, too. Choose cuts with some fat on them to keep the meat moist and succulent.

INGREDIENTS

2/3 cup soy sauce	2 garlic cloves, crushed
3 tablespoons tomato ketchup	1 tablespoon ginger wine or sweet sherry
1 teaspoon brown sugar	1 teaspoon salt
3 tablespoons hoisin sauce	2-pound loin or shoulder of pork, cut into 3-inch long strips

METHOD

■ Mix all the ingredients in a large bowl and marinate the meat for at least 4 hours or overnight. Turn it a couple of times so the liquid soaks in.

■ Preheat the oven to 425° F. Place the pork strips in the oven on a grill rack or oven rack with a foil-lined pan underneath to catch the drips.

■ Roast for 15 minutes, then lower the heat to 350° F. and cook for another 10 to 15 minutes, or until cooked through, but still very moist and succulent in the middle. Ovens vary in temperature, so keep an eye on this and adjust the timing according to your own oven.

■ Brush the meat with the marinade frequently and turn over so all sides get a baked-on coating of sauce.

■ Remove from the oven, slice, and serve with freshly boiled rice, cucumber batons (page 67) and carrot sticks, a vegetable stir-fry, and a range of dips including *Nam Prik* (page 24).

VARIATIONS

■ Hoisin sauce is widely available and does add a special flavor. If you cannot get hold of it, substitute the same quantity of honey, 1 teaspoon lemon juice, and 1 teaspoon ground cinnamon.

■ We have also used lamb ribs for this dish very successfully. Remove as much fat as possible and only use the meaty parts of a breast of lamb.

Tiger Lily Sweet & Sour Pork Ribs

SERVES 3 TO 4

What a glorious animal a pig is. We utilize every part of it except the squeal. It is particularly popular in China and the countries that border the Pacific Rim because its tender meat is ideal for quick stir-frying. It is also easy to keep and you often see pigs rooting around villages alongside of dogs. Many countries, like Malaysia and Indonesia, are Muslim and, naturally, pork is not eaten there. However, the Christians and Chinese have adapted local recipes to suit their favorite meat.

American spareribs, or Chinese ribs, come from the belly of the pig. We usually try to buy the whole belly cut—the meaty ribs we cook in sweet and sour sauce, the thicker lean flank is good for turning into barbecued *Char Sui* (page 98) strips, while the fattier meat and skin make excellent sweet-and-sour pork. Mother used to cut the fat and skin into small pieces, fry them slowly in a wok to crisp, then drain off the excess oil to use for frying or roasting potatoes. The crispy skin left behind would be used to add a delicious crunchy texture to stir-fried dishes.

For this recipe, ask your butcher to cut the ribs into manageable portions, or use a cleaver yourself.

INGREDIENTS

1 quantity Tiger Lily's Special Sweet & Sour Sauce (page 26)	2 pounds spareribs, cut into bite-sized pieces
2 tablespoons soy sauce	1 teaspoon oil (sesame, if possible)

METHOD

- Preheat the oven to 400° F.

- Mix the sweet-and-sour sauce with the soy sauce in a large bowl and marinate the ribs for at least 4 hours or overnight.

- Place the ribs in a shallow baking tray, brush with a little oil, then cook for about 20 minutes.

- Reduce the heat to 350° F. and cook for an additional 30 minutes. Turn the ribs over with tongs a few times during cooking, and baste with leftover marinade.

- Serve hot with boiled rice.

Burmese Pork Curry with Straw Mushrooms

SERVES 4 TO 6

A dry spicy curry, this dish is rich and dark, but with an interesting extra—little straw mushrooms.

INGREDIENTS

1 pound boneless shoulder of pork, not too lean, cut into 2-inch cubes

1/2 teaspoon ground red pepper

1/2 teaspoon ground turmeric

1 teaspoon salt

2 medium onions, chopped

1 stalk lemongrass, crushed, or the rind and juice of 1 lemon

2 garlic cloves, chopped

1 teaspoon sliced chopped galangal or ginger, peeled and cut into very thin shreds

2 small fresh red or green chiles, chopped

1/4 teaspoon *blachan* (shrimp paste) or 1/2 teaspoon dried shrimp

2 tablespoons tamarind juice (1 1/2 teaspoons tamarind pulp mixed with 1 tablespoon water and strained)

2 tablespoons oil

12 ounces canned straw mushrooms, drained

1 teaspoon ground dried shrimp (optional)

METHOD

■ Prick the meat all over with a skewer, put it in a bowl, and mix with the dry spices and salt. Put aside to marinate for about 2 hours.

■ Put the onions, lemongrass, garlic, galangal or ginger, chiles, blachan or dried shrimp, and tamarind juice into a blender and process to a purée.

■ Heat the oil in a pan and add the purée. Cook, stirring constantly, until the liquid evaporates, the mixture begins to fry, and the oil starts to separate out.

■ Add the pork and fry in its own juice for 15 to 20 minutes, or until the meat is cooked. Keep stirring and add a little water to prevent it from burning, if necessary.

■ Stir in the straw mushrooms, and ground dried shrimp if using, simmer for 5 minutes, and serve.

VARIATION

The soft, creamy straw mushrooms make a pleasant contrast to the spicy meat. If they are not available, you can substitute any canned mushrooms.

Chinese Stir-Fried Lamb with Onions

SERVES 4

This is a very delicious, quick and easy family favorite.

INGREDIENTS

12 ounces lamb tenderloin, sliced very thinly across the grain	2 tablespoons vegetable oil
1 teaspoon sugar	1 garlic clove, crushed
1 teaspoon salt	1 teaspoon grated ginger
1 tablespoon soy sauce	2 medium onions, sliced
1 tablespoon cornstarch	1 teaspoon crushed black peppercorns
	1/2 teaspoon sesame oil

METHOD

■ Put the lamb in a bowl and mix with the sugar, salt, soy sauce, and cornstarch.

■ Heat the vegetable oil in a wok until it smokes. Add the garlic and ginger and stir for a few seconds just to flavor the oil.

■ Add the onions and crushed peppercorns and stir until the onions are just cooked. Remove from the heat and set aside.

■ Heat the sesame oil in the wok (do not bring to a smoking heat, as this destroys some of the delicate flavor), add the meat, and stir-fry for 3 minutes or until the lamb is no longer pink. Take care not to overcook.

■ Add the onions and 2 tablespoons water and stir until the sauce becomes thick and glossy.

Sri Lankan Lamb & Spinach Curry

SERVES 4

We love this mixture of spinach and lamb—the stunning contrast of dark meat, rich creamy sauce, and green leaves makes it a feast for the eyes as well as the tastebuds. It is simplicity itself to cook if you have some ready-prepared Sri Lankan Curry Sauce in the refrigerator or freezer.

INGREDIENTS

5 tablespoons oil	1 1/2 teaspoons Garam Masala (page 18)
1 pound shoulder of lamb, cut into 1-inch cubes	1 teaspoon maldive fish or ground dried shrimp
1/4 recipe Sri Lankan Curry Sauce (page 22)	1 pound canned or frozen puréed spinach
1 teaspoon salt	2 teaspoons finely chopped coriander (cilantro) leaves
1/2 to 1 teaspoon ground red pepper (according to taste)	

METHOD

■ Heat the oil in a large saucepan, add the lamb, and fry until just browned (about 5 minutes).

■ Add the curry sauce, 1 1/2 cups water, and the rest of the ingredients, except the spinach and coriander leaves. Bring to a boil, then lower the heat, and simmer for about 15 minutes, or until the curry thickens. Stir constantly to prevent burning.

■ Add the spinach and stir gently to heat through for a few minutes only.

■ Stir in the chopped coriander leaves just before serving.

VARIATION

Add a finely chopped green chile and a swirl (about 2 tablespoons) of thick yogurt with the coriander leaves at step 4.

Lamb Kebobs in Coriander and Mint, with Lemon Yogurt

SERVES 4

Use a boned shoulder or leg of lamb for this sensational dish, which makes a superb alternative to steak and hamburgers for barbecues. Prepare the kebobs the day before and keep refrigerated, covered in plastic wrap.

INGREDIENTS

1 pound boneless lamb, cut into 1-inch cubes	1 tablespoon lemon juice
2 teaspoons mint sauce	1 1/2 cups thick low-fat yogurt
1 tablespoon freshly chopped mint	1 tablespoon oil
1 1/2 teaspoons salt	2 tablespoons melted butter, to brush on kebobs
1 teaspoon freshly ground black pepper	2 lemons (choose the thin-skinned ones)
1 teaspoon ground coriander	

METHOD

■ Start the night before. Put the meat in a bowl with 1 teaspoon of the mint sauce, 1 teaspoon of the chopped fresh mint, the salt, pepper, and coriander, 1 teaspoon of the lemon juice, 2 tablespoons of yogurt, and the oil. Mix well and cover with plastic wrap. Store in the refrigerator overnight.

■ Thread the meat on bamboo sticks (soaked in water for 30 minutes so they do not burn) or on metal skewers.

■ Mix the melted butter with the rest of the lemon juice and use to baste the kebobs.

■ Barbecue or cook under a preheated broiler until cooked through (about 30 minutes), brushing with butter and lemon juice, and turning over halfway through the cooking time.

■ Meanwhile, wash the lemons and cut one into wedges for decoration. Cut the other lemon into pieces and remove as many seeds as you can. Put the seeded lemon into a food processor and process until finely chopped. Put the chopped lemon into a bowl and mix with the remaining mint, mint sauce, and yogurt.

■ Serve the kebobs on a large platter decorated with fresh mint leaves and lemon wedges, rice or Quick and Easy *Naan* Bread (page 80). Accompany with the lemon yogurt and *Sambol Ulek* (page 25) or one of the chile sauces.

103

Mongolian Steamboat or Hot Pot

SERVES 4

A great specialty of the north of China is Mongolian Hot Pork, or Steamboat. This all-in-one dish is made at the dinner table in a metal pan which looks like a miniature stove, with a chimney running through it. Coals are lit in the bottom to keep the flavored stock in the pan at a rolling boil. Guests sit around the pot with a supply of raw shrimp, scallops, fish, squid, chicken, lamb, beef, *pak choi* (Chinese cabbage), bean sprouts, cellophane noodles, and scallions handy. They use chopsticks to drop in whatever meat or vegetables they fancy and each has a small metal basket on a long handle to fish out the cooked ingredients, dip them in a range of sauces, and eat them immediately.

The stock becomes richer and more flavorful as the evening progresses. Finally, when all the meat and vegetables are gone, the noodles are added and eaten with some of the soup.

Try our simplified version of this great dish, using lamb. As Steamboat involves almost instant cooking, if you use beef you need to use the best, most tender cuts. And it is not necessary to own a steamboat to enjoy this dish. A saucepan over a high heat will do.

INGREDIENTS

8 ounces boneless lamb	4 ounces spinach, washed and torn into large pieces (2 cups)
3 1/2 cups Homemade Chicken Stock (page 29) or 2 Knorr chicken stock cubes dissolved in the same quantity of boiling water	1 cup bamboo shoots, cut into shreds
	1 cup bean sprouts, washed
1/2 teaspoon salt (optional)	4 ounces cellophane noodles, cut with scissors into 2-inch pieces, soaked in hot water for 30 minutes before use, then drained
1/3 cup sliced water chestnuts	

METHOD

■ Cut the lamb into paper-thin 1-inch squares.

■ Put the stock in a pan and bring to a boil. Taste and add the salt only if necessary.

■ Drop the ingredients in and boil for 3 minutes only, or until the lamb loses its pinkness. Take care not to overcook.

■ Serve in bowls with chopsticks and soup spoons, with a selection of sauces, including Vietnamese Dipping Sauce (page 25) and *Sambol Ulek* (page 25).

POULTRY

▲▲▲▲▲▲▲▲▲▲▲▲▲▲▲▲

Poor old chickens are the most unfortunate creatures in the world. Everyone (other than vegetarians) enjoys eating them and their eggs, and every village in Southeast Asia has flocks of colorful fowl scratching in the dust and scattering, squawking, and complaining, at the approach of cars or little children who find endless pleasure in chasing them! Our chickens are yellow and full of flavor when cooked, but tend to be tougher than the large, flabby, tender, but tasteless white fowl available in the West. We always go for a boiling fowl for curries (utterly delicious) and a free-range or corn-fed bird for quick cooking or roasting.

Incidentally, do not throw away the fat that you find in the body cavity or under the breast in a roasting or boiling chicken. Instead, cut the fat into small pieces and slowly heat it in a pan until it melts. This fat can be kept in a refrigerator for up to three weeks. It makes excellent roast potatoes and also adds a special flavor to stir-fried dishes.

When we were young, Mother used to keep chickens and we once—aged four and six—broke our hearts and cried with remorse after innocently drowning half a dozen fluffy yellow chicks in the bath. We thought they needed the yolk cleaned off them, but our pudgy little hands squeezed them so tightly they had no chance of survival. The product of strict Methodist grandparents, we insisted they were given proper funerals with tiny flower garlands and hymns, and grieved for quite some time.

Ducks are very popular in China, and racks upon racks of the shiny mahogany brown fowl are seen hanging in restaurant windows in the Orient, tempting passersby with their wonderful aroma. One of our favorite meals is duck rice—a plate of steaming white rice topped with pieces of barbecued duck, plain steamed *pak choi* or some other green vegetable, and soy sauce.

The triumphant crow of a cock, followed by the raucous cawing of crows, used to wake us each morning, whether in town, city, or village. In Hong Kong, where space is at a premium, people even keep chickens in high-rise apartment buildings!

Easy Sweet & Sour Chicken with Bamboo Shoots & Cashew Nuts

SERVES 3 TO 4

This is a recipe for those "do I really have to cook?" days. If you are handy with a knife and a can opener you can have this on the table within 10 minutes. It is perfect if you assemble all the ingredients the night before, and leave them in the refrigerator, covered with plastic wrap. Then, after a hard day at the office, a quick zap in the wok produces instant Oriental magic.

INGREDIENTS

1/2 teaspoon salt	1 garlic clove, crushed
2 teaspoons cornstarch	1 1/2-inch piece of fresh ginger, peeled and crushed
2 large chicken breasts, weighing approximately 1 pound, sliced into thin strips	1/2 recipe Tiger Lily's Special Sweet & Sour Sauce (page 26) *or* 1 tablespoon hoisin sauce, 1 tablespoon tomato ketchup, and 1 teaspoon soy sauce
2 tablespoons oil	
1/2 cup canned bamboo shoots	
1 red or green bell pepper, cut into 1-inch squares	1 tablespoon ginger wine or sweet sherry
1 small onion, finely sliced	3/4 cup roasted salted cashew nuts

METHOD

■ Mix the salt and cornstarch together, add the chicken, and mix together.

■ Heat a wok and add the oil. When it begins to smoke, add the chicken and stir-fry for 3 minutes. Remove the chicken with a slotted spoon, drain on paper towels, and keep warm.

■ Put the rest of the ingredients in the wok, except and sweet and sour sauce (or alternative seasonings), the ginger wine or sherry, and the cashew nuts. Stir-fry for about 3 minutes, then add the cooked chicken, sweet and sour sauce (or alternative seasonings), ginger wine or sherry, and heat through.

■ Stir in the cashew nuts and serve with boiled rice.

VARIATION

Add a handful of chopped water chestnuts, fresh bean sprouts, or sticks of cucumber to the wok with the sherry at step 3. These should all stay crisp and only be lightly stir-fried for not more than 2 minutes.

Chicken Batons

MAKES 20 TO
24; ENOUGH
FOR 4 TO 6 AS
A STARTER OR
10 TO 15 AS
PART OF A
BUFFET

A fun starter but good for party buffets, too. Wrap a small piece of aluminum foil around the end of the bone to make it less messy to pick up. Chicken wings are cheap and easily available. Choose small ones for this recipe. They are perfect for a mouthful, and you can prepare them a day in advance. All you need is a chopping board and a sharp knife.

Make at least twice as many as you would expect any normal person to eat—they disappear like magic.

INGREDIENTS

2 pounds chicken wings	2 eggs
2 cups self-rising flour	1 teaspoon sesame oil
3/4 cup cornstarch	Salt and pepper
1/2 teaspoon salt	1 quart oil, for deep-frying

METHOD

■ Cut the wing into 3 pieces at the joints (see below). Discard the wing tips or use them to make Homemade Chicken Stock (page 29).

■ Take the 2 remaining portions and, using a knife, loosen the meat from the bone and pull it down to the end of the joint. When you get to the end, pull it right over the bone and tuck in to form a ball. Imagine the bone is your leg and you are rolling a stocking down it, and bunching it around your foot! It should end up looking like a mini toffee apple. (See below).

■ The joint nearest the wing tip has 2 bones—work one bone free, cut through the tendon and discard the bone. You will end up with a plateful of what looks like mini drum batons.

■ To make the batter, put the flour, cornstarch, and 1/2 teaspoon salt in a mixing bowl with the eggs and sesame oil. Add just under 3/4 cup water and beat together until it becomes a thick cream.

■ Salt and pepper the chicken batons, then dip them into the batter. Shake off the excess.

■ Heat the cooking oil in a wok or deep-fryer until it begins to smoke, then drop in the batons, and fry until cooked through, or for about 5 to 8 minutes, depending on the size of the pieces. Cook in 2 to 3 batches, depending on the size of your wok. Drain on paper towels, and serve with Tiger Lily's Special Sweet & Sour Sauce (page 26), Satay Sauce (page 28), or any chile sauce.

VARIATION

Place 3/4 cup lightly toasted sesame seeds in a bowl beside the sauces. Guests take a baton, dip it in the sauce of their choice and then in the sesame seeds before eating.

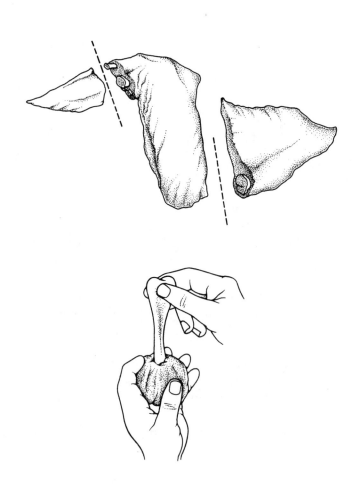

Barbecued Duck

SERVES 4 TO 6; ENOUGH FOR A 3- TO 3 1/2-POUND DUCK OR CHICKEN, 2 POUNDS CHINESE SPARERIBS, OR 1 LARGE FISH

We traveled extensively around the world when we were young, rarely staying longer than two or three years in any one spot. We took few possessions with us, but one that we have always had, which has ended up in Rani's kitchen, is a dark stone mortar and pestle from Thailand.

When we were posted to England in 1955, our servants and cook refused to accompany us—they had heard about the cold, wet English weather and were not prepared to leave beautiful tropical Sri Lanka!

Mum was a hopeless cook. Having always been surrounded by domestic help, she couldn't even boil rice, let alone an egg. In the early days, we shared a flat with a family in Bromley until we found permanent accommodation, and their mother had to give Mum a hand or we would have starved.

After a month of unrelieved bacon and mashed potato pie and English roasts, we all rebelled, and Mum was forced to invent something. Out came and mortar and pestle, and ginger and garlic were pounded with soy sauce, sugar, vinegar, and sherry until they formed a paste, which was then rubbed on just about anything—from chops to chicken—before roasting.

Amazingly, this mix has survived to this day, although we are now more inclined to save work and use a blender to blend the ingredients. You can store the sauce in the refrigerator in an airtight container for up to 4 days.

INGREDIENTS

2 garlic cloves	1 1/2 teaspoons rice wine vinegar
4 slices fresh ginger, peeled	1 tablespoon sweet sherry
1 tablespoon soy sauce	1 tablespoon salt
1 tablespoon honey or sugar	3-pound to 3 1/2-pound duck

METHOD

■ Pound the garlic and ginger in a mortar and pestle, then add the liquid ingredients and salt to make a sauce. Or put all the ingredients in a blender and blend until completely smooth. It can be used as a rub, a marinade, or in stir-fries.

■ For barbecued duck, leave the duck to marinate in the sauce for at least 4 hours or overnight, turning frequently to let the flavors sink in.

■ Preheat the oven to 375° F. Put the bird on its breast and roast for 1 hour, basting occasionally with the marinade and juices in the pan.

■ Reduce the temperature to 300° F., turn the bird onto its back and cook for another 45 minutes. Baste again.

■ If needed, add 1 tablespoon water to the pan to stop the juices burning. Plunge a skewer into the bird between the thigh and body (where the meat is thickest). If the juice runs clear, the duck is done; if not, cook until it does run clear. The skin should be a deep mahogany color. If not, turn the temperature up to 375° F. and roast until it browns.

VARIATIONS

■ Try adding one or some of the following ingredients, but also think up some of your own:

INGREDIENTS

2 small fresh green chiles, chopped	2 slices galangal instead of the ginger
1 tablespoon peanut butter	1 tablespoon fresh coriander (cilantro) leaves
1 tablespoon ginger wine instead of the sherry	

Paper-Wrapped Chicken & Snowpeas

SERVES 4 TO 6

This next recipe must be the only low-calorie, healthy, deep-fried one you will ever come across. It looks very spectacular and is ideal for entertaining, as it can be prepared the day before, then fried just before serving.

INGREDIENTS

3 scallions, washed, trimmed, and finely shredded, or a 2-inch piece of galangal, peeled and cut into thin matchsticks	1 teaspoon hoisin sauce
	20 to 24 snowpeas
2 tablespoons soy sauce	2 chicken breast fillets, approximately 12 ounces, cut into 20 to 24 pieces
1 tablespoon rice wine or sweet sherry	
1 teaspoon sugar	2 teaspoons sesame oil
	4 cups oil, for deep-frying

METHOD

■ Marinate the scallions or galangal in a bowl with the soy sauce, rice wine or sherry, sugar, hoisin sauce, snowpeas, and chicken for 20 minutes.

■ Prepare 20 to 24 squares of 6-inch waxed or greaseproof paper. Brush each piece of paper on one side with a little sesame oil. Put it on a flat surface, oiled side up, with a corner facing you. It should look like a diamond. Put a little scallion or galangal, a piece of chicken, then a pea pod in the middle of the paper.

■ Bring up the bottom corner to cover the ingredients. Now fold over the right corner, then the left, over the ingredients. Bring the top corner down towards you, then tuck it into the flap made by the folded corners. This is the same method used for Stuffed Spring Rolls (page 48).

■ Heat the oil in a wok until it begins to smoke. Deep-fry the packages, a few at a time, for 2 minutes on each side. When all the packages are cooked, bring the oil up to smoking point and re-fry in 2 batches for another minute to reheat thoroughly. Drain on paper towels.

■ Place on a serving dish with a selection of chile sauces and Vietnamese Dipping Sauce (page 25). Guests open each package at the table and dunk the contents in the dipping sauce before eating.

VARIATION

You can use the same method with whole giant fresh shrimp, or fillets of good-quality white fish.

Indonesian Grilled Spicy Chicken

SERVES 3 TO 4

This is a delicious alternative to plain grilled chicken and is also very good for barbecues. A lovely buttery crust develops on the surface of the chicken and it looks and smells mouth-watering. Eat this with rice, Quick and Easy *Naan* Bread (page 80), Coconut Rotis (page 74) or other Asian dishes, or really surprise everyone by serving it with garlic bread, green salad, and potato salad.

This is an ideal dish for a dinner party. You can prepare the chicken to step 5 and keep it cool for up to 6 hours before serving. Then finish the dish with step 6, and serve.

INGREDIENTS

3- to 3 1/2-pound chicken	1 cup coconut milk
1 medium onion, chopped	1/2 teaspoon ground black pepper
3 garlic cloves, chopped	1/4 teaspoon ground turmeric
2 fresh red chiles, chopped	1 1/2 teaspoons salt
1 teaspoon crushed fresh ginger	2 tablespoons melted butter or ghee
1 stalk of lemongrass, crushed, or the grated rind of 1 lemon	Juice of 1 lemon

METHOD

▪ Cut the chicken in half lengthways. Make deep horizontal cuts in the flesh, rinse with clean water, and dry with paper towels.

▪ Put the onion, garlic, chiles, ginger, and lemongrass or lemon rind in a blender with 1 tablespoon water and blend to a paste. Add the coconut milk.

▪ Mix the pepper, turmeric, and salt together and rub over the chicken, going deep into the cuts.

▪ Put the coconut mixture in a wok, bring slowly to a boil, and add the chicken. Simmer for 20 minutes, or until the water evaporates, turning the chicken once or twice.

▪ Remove the chicken from the wok and keep to one side. Add the melted butter or ghee and the lemon juice to the wok.

▪ When ready to serve, preheat a broiler and brown the chicken on both sides, basting it with the spicy lemon-butter juices from the wok. This should take 10 to 15 minutes. Serve on a bed of watercress.

EGGS

▲▲▲▲▲▲▲▲▲▲▲▲▲▲▲▲▲

Because ducks and hens are so widely raised in Asia, eggs are eaten frequently. Duck eggs are much prized, especially in China. But ducks are natural scavengers so their eggs require long, thorough cooking in order to kill any salmonella harbored in the rich, deep yellow yolks. They make wonderful Sweet Sour Eggs.

Hen's eggs are more readily available. The Chinese boil and cook them red (in soy sauce) or stir beaten egg into a hot dish before taking it off the heat. This is just long enough for the egg to begin to coagulate and form thin threads, as in Egg Drop Soup.

In Indonesia, Sri Lanka, and other countries, omelets are very popular. Sometimes they are flavored with onions, chiles, sugar, and spices or made more substantial with the addition of shrimp or some other seafood.

One of our favorite breakfasts of all time is Mock Stringhoppers, *Hodi*, Coconut Sambol, and plain omelet. A meal fit for a queen!

Sweet & Sour Eggs with Red-Braised Pork

SERVES 6 TO 8

Everyone loves sweet and sour pork, but when we were children we would overlook the tender meat in this dish in favor of the dark brown savory eggs, deeply slashed to show a streak of golden yolk. Eaten with rice, Mum's special carrot pickle, and quick fried beans, this was as close to heaven as we could get.

Sweet-and-sour eggs make good party food. Simply follow the recipe but omit the pork. Carefully cut each egg into four segments and serve on a bed of shredded lettuce decorated with carved vegetable flowers (page 124).

INGREDIENTS

1 pound fatty pork (a belly cut is good, with the rind and fat)	3/4 cup soy sauce
8 hard-boiled eggs, shelled	1 tablespoon brown sugar
2 tablespoons oil	2 teaspoons salt
1 garlic clove, crushed	3 tablespoons rice wine
1 large onion, chopped	4 tablespoons sweet sherry
2 slices ginger, peeled and crushed	1 star anise (optional)

METHOD

■ Cut the pork into 2-inch cubes. Place each egg on a chopping board, holding it steady with one hand. Then, with a sharp knife, make deep vertical cuts all around the egg. Do not make the cuts too close to each other—all you are trying to do is let the rich sauce sink into the heart of the egg.

■ Heat the oil in a pan with a lid, then fry the garlic, onion, and ginger until the onion softens. Add the pork and stir-fry until it begins to brown.

■ Put all the ingredients, except the eggs, into a deep pan with a lid. Add 1/2 cup water, cover, and bring to a boil.

■ Carefully add the eggs, moving the pork chunks to one side so that all the eggs are under the sauce.

■ Simmer for about 1 hour. Very gently turn the eggs during cooking so that they are evenly covered with the sauce. It will gradually reduce and get very thick. When done, the meat becomes meltingly tender.

■ Place the meat and eggs in a dish, serve, and wait for the compliments.

Egg Curry

SERVES 4 TO 6

A great dish—much underrated we feel. In our version, the eggs are rubbed with spices, then fried to seal the surface, and finally cooked gently in a mild curry sauce.

INGREDIENTS

6 hard-boiled eggs, shelled

1 teaspoon ground turmeric

1 to 2 teaspoons salt

2 1/2 cups oil, for deep-frying

1 medium onion, sliced

2 slices ginger, peeled and chopped

2 garlic cloves, crushed

1 teaspoon grated maldive fish or dried shrimp (optional)

4 curry leaves (optional)

2-inch piece *rampe* (pandanus leaf, optional)

1/4 teaspoon ground cinnamon

1/2 teaspoon ground red pepper

1/4 teaspoon ground coriander

1/2 teaspoon ground cumin

1/2 teaspoon ground mixed spice

1 tomato, sliced

Juice and rind of 1/2 lime

1/4 cup coconut milk

A pinch of Garam Masala (page 18)

METHOD

■ Prick the eggs all over with a metal skewer to stop them from bursting when they are fried. Rub with the turmeric and salt.

■ Heat the oil in a wok and deep-fry the eggs until they are a golden brown. Put the eggs in a dish and keep the oil on one side.

■ Put the onion, ginger, and garlic in a blender with 2/3 cup water and blend to a paste.

■ Drain off all the oil from the wok except for 2 tablespoons and fry the onion paste, and maldive fish or dried shrimp, curry leaves, and *rampe* if using, until they begin to brown.

■ Add all the ingredients, except the eggs, coconut milk, and garam masala. Bring to a boil, and simmer for 15 minutes, or until the sauce begins to thicken.

■ Add the eggs, coconut milk, and 3/4 cup water and simmer for another 5 to 10 minutes. Stir in a pinch of garam masala to taste, and serve.

VARIATION

Alternatively, follow steps 1 and 2, then add 1/4 recipe Sri Lankan Curry Sauce (page 22) to 2 tablespoons of the oil used to fry the eggs. Add the eggs, coconut milk, 3/4 cup water, and adjust the seasoning. Simmer for 10 minutes, and serve.

Indonesian Spicy Omelet

SERVES 2 TO 3

Ever since someone hit on the notion of breaking an egg and frying it in oil, happy eaters around the world have dug into variations on the omelet. The Spanish make a deep omelet with peppers and onions, which is cut into wedges like a cake. Chinese omelets are flavored with the mushrooms, crabmeat, and scallions and usually fried in sesame oil. In Southeast Asia, the most popular ingredients are chiles and onions, as in this recipe from Indonesia.

INGREDIENTS

4 eggs
1/2 teaspoon salt
1 teaspoon soy sauce

1/2 teaspoon jaggery (palm sugar) or brown sugar
1 tablespoon oil
2 fresh green or red chiles, finely chopped

METHOD

■ Beat the eggs until frothy, then add the salt, soy sauce, and sugar.

■ Heat the oil in a frying pan. Fry the onions until brown, add the chiles and stir for a few seconds. Spread the mixture evenly over the pan.

■ Pour the eggs over the onion mixture. Cook over a low heat until the top begins to set and the bottom is brown.

■ Place on a warmed plate, and serve.

VARIATION

One-half cup crabmeat or fresh peeled shrimp can be added to the beaten eggs at step 1 to make a more substantial dish.

Golden Coin Eggs

SERVES 4

This recipe is so called because the folded eggs look like silk purses containing golden coins. Served with *chok* or Chinese watery rice, this was one of our favorite childhood meals. Mother would get the servants to make this nourishing, easily digested Chinese specialty when we were convalescing from an illness.

INGREDIENTS

1 tablespoon oil	1 1/2 teaspoons tomato ketchup
4 large eggs	1/2 teaspoon sugar
1 tablespoon soy sauce	1/2 teaspoon salt
	1 teaspoon rice wine vinegar

METHOD

■ Heat the oil in a frying pan.

■ Break the eggs into the pan as if making ordinary fried eggs, and cook over a medium heat. When almost set, use a spatula to gently fold each egg in half like a purse. Press gently on the edges to seal.

■ Add the rest of the ingredients to the pan and heat gently.

■ Before the eggs have set solid, carefully slide off onto the bowls of thin *Chok* (page 70).

VARIATION

Serve with soy sauce, chopped scallion, and finely sliced *tung choi* (Chinese preserved vegetable) sprinkled over the top.

FISH AND SEAFOOD

▲▲▲▲▲▲▲▲▲▲▲▲▲▲▲▲

Fish and seafood are a major element in the staple diet of Thais, Malaysians, Sri Lankans, and Indonesians. Anyone with a rod and pole can catch enough fish to feed themselves—the seas and rivers are teeming with a multitude of species that practically leap into the net or basket.

In Sri Lanka, tourists flock to see the pole fisherman, who stand on tiny platforms built on wooden poles far out to sea. Silhouetted against the vivid crimson, emerald, and vermilion hues of a tropical sunset, they are wondrous to behold.

Also popular are the many types of shellfish found in Southeast Asia. Abalone steaks make fine eating, as do the many clams and shellfish. As children, when we were being particularly obnoxious and driving the servants to despair, Mother would give us each a pail and send us to the beach to gather *mutties* (small round clams). We would walk along the beach, feeling the sand with our toes and watching for the bubbles on the tide that showed where they were hiding. We would then pounce and fill our pails in a very short time (too quickly for Mother!). They would find their way into the pot for delicious soup noodles.

Tiger Lily Tamarind Fish

SERVES 4

Because we love eating so much, and were fortunate when young to have parents would could take us out regularly, we made firm friends with several families who ran Chinese restaurants in Sri Lanka. Mother's very good friends were the Suans who owned the Dragon Café in Colombo. All Chinese have a love of gambling, and Mum would go to play Mah Jong with them. It is similar to gin rummy but the players use chunky painted tiles made of bone or plastic. We loved it when the tiles were turned face down at the end of the game and "washed" (shuffled around the table). The noise was terrific as each tile clinked and clanked against its neighbors, and we were sometimes allowed to join in.

The Suans were very generous, wonderful cooks and we first came across a whole baked fish at their Dragon Café. We enjoyed lavish banquets there and we once ate for so long (about four or five hours) that Chandra fell asleep in the middle of the noodles—out like a light.

This recipe is spectacular, although very easy to do. Wait for the "Oooh!" from your guests when the parcel is opened at the table. Invest in a long oval dish (a turkey dish is ideal) so the fish does not flop over the sides!

INGREDIENTS

2 small or one large sea bass, trout, or red snapper, gutted, but with the head left on	2 teaspoons soy sauce
	1 teaspoon rice wine vinegar
2 teaspoons dried tamarind, mixed with a little hot water and strained	1/2 teaspoon crushed fresh ginger
	1/2 teaspoon crushed garlic
1 teaspoon salted black beans	4 scallions, washed, trimmed, and chopped
1 teaspoon sugar	

METHOD

■ Slash the fish deeply on both sides, making parallel diagonal cuts. It looks even better if you heat a metal skewer and press it against the fish several times, going diagonally across the cuts. This branding creates a very attractive diamond pattern.

■ Mix all the ingredients, except the scallions, to a cream, then rub into the fish well, especially inbetween the cuts.

■ Place the fish in a large piece of foil, and sprinkle the chopped scallions on top. Bring the sides of the foil up and form a loose tent at the top, turning the edges over twice to seal. Then bake in a preheated oven, at 425° F., for about 20 minutes.

■ Bring to the table in the foil. When the tent is opened, a wonderful steam cloud of ginger and spices will waft up—very impressive!

VARIATION

The fish can simply be placed on a plate and steamed for the same length of time.

Salt Fish Curry

SERVES 3 TO 4

Although fresh fish is eaten so frequently in Southeast Asia, to add interest and variety to our diet, we also eat salted fish—from small *harl masu* (tiny sprat-like fish) and dried shrimp up to large cutlets from jack or king fish or tuna. We believe salted fish was introduced to Sri Lanka by the Portuguese, perhaps as a way of transporting the abundance of their Southeast Asian territory back home.

This is a dry curry, best served at a lukewarm temperature, with lots of boiled rice or Coconut Rotis (page 74), and, of course, Coconut Sambol (page 30) and Tomato, Cucumber, & Onion Sambol (page 32).

INGREDIENTS

8 ounces salt fish	2 garlic cloves, chopped
2 tablespoons oil	1 1/2 teaspoons grated fresh ginger
1 large onion, chopped	3 curry leaves (optional)
1 tablespoon mustard seeds, ground with a little water	1 tablespoon rice wine vinegar
	1 teaspoon sugar
1 teaspoon ground red pepper	2 tablespoons coconut milk

METHOD

■ Cut the salt fish into small pieces or shreds, heat the oil in a pan, and fry the fish with the onion until both are crisp and beginning to brown.

■ Add the mustard seeds, red pepper, garlic, ginger, and curry leaves, if using, and stir gently for another 1 to 2 minutes.

■ Add the vinegar and sugar with 6 tablespoons water and simmer until all the liquid has gone. Add the coconut milk into the mixture and stir it in.

Jewel Fish in Lemon Sauce

SERVES 4 TO 6

China's Eastern Province's cuisine is similar to the Peking style of cooking. Shanghai is the major town here and, because of its coastal position, the local people tend to eat a lot of fish.

This recipe from Shanghai is for succulent fish in a light batter served with a deliciously different lemon sauce. If you wish, you could substitute chicken breast for the fish. Both are firm favorites of ours. Assemble the ingredients for the sauce, fish, and batter before you start.

INGREDIENTS

SAUCE

4 tablespoons lemon juice

1 teaspoon grated lemon rind

2 teaspoons cornstarch

1 1/4 cups 2 1/4 cups Homemade Chicken Stock (page 29) or 1/2 chicken stock cube dissolved in the same quantity of boiling water

2 scallions, washed, trimmed, and shredded

1/4 teaspoon salt

1 tablespoon honey

FISH

1 pound white fish fillets (e.g., sole or cod, cut into bite-sized strips)

1 tablespoon sherry or rice wine

1 teaspoon salt

3 tablespoons cornstarch

BATTER

1 cup self-rising flour

1/4 teaspoon baking powder

1 egg

2 1/2 cups oil, for deep-frying

METHOD

■ Combine all the sauce ingredients and cook over a low heat until they thicken, stirring all the time. Keep warm.

■ Marinate the fish pieces in the sherry or rice wine and salt for 30 minutes. Then dip each piece in the cornstarch before coating in batter.

■ To prepare the batter, mix the flour, baking powder, and egg with 1/2 cup cold water, and beat well.

■ Meanwhile, bring the oil slowly up to smoking point in a wok or deep-fryer. Dip the pieces of fish in the batter, shake to get rid of any excess, carefully lower into the oil, and deep-fry a few at a time until golden brown. Keep the pieces warm while you fry the rest.

■ To serve, arrange the fish on a platter. Pour over the sauce, then decorate with an assortment of radish water lilies, carrot and scallion knots, scallion tassels, and sweet pepper jewels (see below).

DECORATIVE VEGETABLES

■ To make radish lilies, cut the top of each radish. Then, using a sharp knife but without cutting right through, make 3 deep vertical cuts in the vegetable, forming 6 segments. Soak in cold water until the cuts open out to form lilies.

■ To make carrot knots, wash and peel each carrot, and cut into very thin slices lengthways. Cut each slice into very fine strips or julienne. Take each strip and gently tie into a loose knot. If the carrot is very fresh and brittle and refuses to comply, put the strips into boiling water for a few seconds to make them more pliable.

■ To make scallion knots, cut the long green leaves into strips, then tie into knots.

■ To make scallion tassels, cut most of the green part off (use to make knots), leaving the bulb and about 1 inch of stalk. Using a sharp knife, carefully cut the green leaves into strips almost to the center. Alternatively, cut both ends (the green leaves and the bulb) into strips almost to the center. Put the tassels to soak in a bowl of cold water until they open out.

■ To make pepper jewels, use a selection of green, orange, and red peppers. Remove the seeds and most of the pith. Then cut the flesh into diamond jewel shapes and sprinkle over the fish dish. If you have a steady hand (and the time) you could try cutting the pepper into more ornate shapes, such as stars and octagons, to resemble other gems.

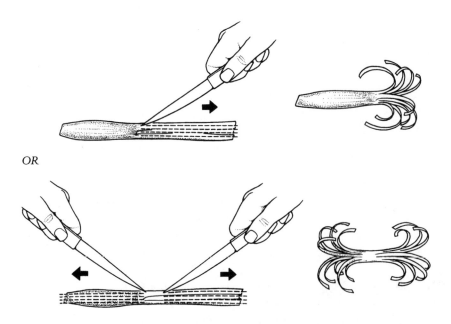

OR

Coconut Fish Curry

SERVES 4

This is a Sri Lankan specialty and very good it is! Hot and spicy but with a creamy sweetness due to the coconut milk.

INGREDIENTS

1 tablespoon ground red pepper	1 pound fish (e.g., cod, hake, tuna, or mackerel), cut into 1-inch chunks
1 teaspoon ground turmeric	1 tablespoon oil
1/4 teaspoon ground cinnamon	1 stalk lemongrass or the juice and grated rind of 1 lemon
3 garlic cloves, crushed	
1 teaspoon grated fresh ginger	2-inch piece of *rampe* (pandanus) (optional)
1 teaspoon celery salt	
1 teaspoon salt	5 curry leaves (optional)
2 onions, chopped	3/4 cup coconut milk

METHOD

■ Mix the red pepper, turmeric, cinnamon, garlic, ginger, celery salt, salt, and onions in a large bowl. Rub the fish with this mixture and set aside for 15 minutes to let the flavors penetrate.

■ Heat the oil in a saucepan and fry the lemongrass (or lemon rind), and *rampe* and curry leaves, if using, for a few seconds. Take the fish out of the bowl and add it to the pan. Fry until golden brown, taking care not to let the pieces break up.

■ Add the remaining spice mixture in the bowl to the pan, along with the coconut milk. Simmer until the curry is cooked. Stir in the lemon juice, if using, and serve.

Deep-fried Sprats with Spicy Dipping Sauce

SERVES 4

In Sri Lanka and Malaysia, we used to be enthralled by all the little fish which darted in and out of the rock formations in the thousands, like brilliantly colored, billowing clouds. We confess that we ate neon and angel fish, gold and black guppies and other aquarium favorite without any qualms—they were caught in the fishermen's nets in such profusion.

INGREDIENTS

3 tablespoons soy sauce	2 teaspoons salt
2 tablespoons sherry	1/2 teaspoon ground red pepper
1 teaspoon finely grated fresh ginger	2 tablespoons cornstarch
1 pound small fish, e.g., whitebait, sprats, or sardines (or empty the aquarium if you have tired of them—only joking!)	2 1/2 cups oil, for deep-frying

METHOD

■ Prepare the sauce by mixing the soy sauce, sherry, and ginger in a saucepan. Bring it to a boil, then allow it to get cold.

■ If the fish are very small there is no need to take off their heads or gut them. Those who are more squeamish can do both. Wash them and dry thoroughly on paper towels.

■ Sprinkle with the salt and red pepper and leave for 30 minutes.

■ Put the cornstarch in a paper or plastic bag. Then put in a few fish at a time and gently shake them until they are lightly covered. Place on a plate and repeat until all the fish are coated.

■ Bring the oil to smoking point in a wok or deep-frying, and fry the fish in batches until they are crisp and brown.

■ Serve with the dipping sauce, *Sambol Ulek* (page 25), and thin slices of lime.

Sri Lankan Fish Balls

SERVES 4

INGREDIENTS

1-pound can salmon or tuna, drained	1 garlic clove, crushed
1 small onion, finely chopped	1 teaspoon finely crushed ginger
2 small green chiles, chopped	1 teaspoon lime juice
1 teaspoon salt	2 eggs
1/2 teaspoon ground black pepper	3 tablespoons flour
1 teaspoon ground coriander	4 cups fresh bread crumbs
1 teaspoon ground cumin	2 1/2 cups oil, for deep-frying
1 large potato, weighing about 8 ounces, peeled, boiled, and mashed	

METHOD

■ Mix all the ingredients, except one egg and the flour, bread crumbs, and oil, in a bowl. Roll into small balls about the size of a large marble or walnut.

■ Break the other egg into a bowl and whisk lightly with a fork. Put the flour and bread crumbs into two separate bowls. Line them up on a work surface in this order—flour, egg, bread crumbs, then a large empty plate. You are about to start a production line!

■ Roll the fish balls in the flour, then the egg, then the bread crumbs, and put them on the plate. Use up all the fish mixture this way.

■ Heat the oil to its smoking point in a deep-fryer or wok and fry the balls until golden brown, not too many at a time. This will ensure that the oil stays hot and the balls remain crispy. Garnish with parsley or coriander (cilantro) leaves on a bed of shredded lettuce and serve with Tamarind & Date Dip (page 40) and *Sambol Ulek* (page 25).

Cheena Patas Shrimp

CHINESE FIRECRACKER SHRIMP

SERVES 4 TO 6 **O**ur mother was a Chinese film star, known as a beauty in her day. In fact, she was once walking in London's Soho with my father when she was accosted by a gray-haired old man outside a cinema club (no, not one of those, but one that shows Chinese films exclusively). He had recognized our mother—not bad as she had left the film world in her early thirties and at the time of the encounter she was a mere 81!

When we lived in Sri Lanka, she was plagued by gangs of little boys who would pull the corners of their eyes up with their fingers and shout "*Cheena nona*" (Chinese lady). This enraged both her and our driver, who needed little encouragement to leg it after them, scattering oaths and backhand swipes. It was all good fun and the boys would run away laughing hysterically, while Mother shook her umbrella at them.

This recipe always reminds us of Mom—a firecracker if ever there was one. *Patas* means "bang" in Malay and the frying shrimp do sound a bit like crackers going off.

INGREDIENTS

2 large onions, finely chopped	2 pounds shrimp in their shells
2 garlic cloves, finely chopped	1 teaspoon ground red pepper
2 tablespoons oil	3 tablespoons tomato ketchup
2 teaspoons salt	1 tablespoon lemon juice

METHOD

■ Fry the onions and garlic in the oil until they begin to color.

■ Add the salt and shrimp and stir.

■ Add the rest of the ingredients and fry until they are well blended and the oil begins to separate around the edge of the pan.

■ Serve on a bed of fluffy white rice.

Sour Shrimp Curry with Tamarind

SERVES 4 TO 6

An easy-to-make Thai specialty—juicy whole shrimp in a clear, hot and spicy sauce.

INGREDIENTS

1 pound raw shrimp	3 tablespoons fish sauce
1 tablespoon diced fresh garlic	4 teaspoons tamarind, mixed with 3 tablespoons hot water and strained
1 tablespoon chopped scallions	
1 teaspoon *blachan* (shrimp paste)	2 fresh red chiles, chopped

METHOD

- Clean the shrimp. Take off the heads and shells and remove and discard the dark line running down the back of each one.

- Put the heads and shells into a pan with 3 cups water and boil for 10 minutes. Strain and keep the liquid.

- Pound the garlic and scallions to a paste, or use an electric blender.

- Add the rest of the ingredients, except the chiles, to the shrimp stock and simmer gently for 5 minutes until the shrimp are cooked. Do not overcook or they will toughen and lose their succulence.

- Stir in the chopped chiles and serve.

Sri Lankan Shrimp Curry

SERVES 4 TO 6

In Sri Lanka we have an amazing range of shrimp, from tiny, threadlike ones to huge monsters, some 1 pound in weight. Negombo Lagoon tiger shrimp are highly prized for their sweetness and succulence. Their name comes from the dark tiger-like stripes on their shells. For this recipe, you need to buy the biggest, best-quality shrimp you can find.

INGREDIENTS

1 large onion, chopped	1/4 recipe Sri Lankan Curry Sauce (page 22)
1 garlic clove, crushed	
2 tablespoons oil	2 medium-sized potatoes, peeled and cut into very small cubes
1 teaspoon crushed maldive fish or dried shrimp (optional)	2 kaffir lime leaves (optional)
1 pound shrimp (raw or the best-quality frozen)	

METHOD

■ Fry the onion and garlic in the oil until they begin to turn brown.

■ Add the maldive fish or dried shrimp, if using, and stir for a few seconds more.

■ Add the shrimp, curry sauce, 3/4 cup water, potatoes, and lime leaves, if using. Bring to a boil, then reduce the heat, and simmer for 10 to 15 minutes, or until the potatoes are cooked.

VARIATIONS

■ If you prefer a creamier curry, add a little coconut milk at the end of the cooking time.

■ If a sweeter curry is more to your taste, stir in 1 teaspoon paprika, 1 tablespoon tomato purée, and 2 chopped tomatoes with the potato at step 3.

Lobster Cantonese

SERVES 4 TO 6

A classic recipe. Nothing beats the taste of a freshly boiled lobster, so if you are lucky enough to be given the choice, always go for a fresh one.

INGREDIENTS

Two 1-pound lobsters, freshly boiled	3 tablespoons oil
1 tablespoon soy sauce	1 teaspoon crushed ginger
1 teaspoon sherry	2 garlic cloves, crushed
1 teaspoon sugar	2 tablespoons black beans, soaked in water then crushed (optional)
1/2 teaspoon salt	4 ounces ground pork (1/2 cup)
1/2 cup 2 1/4 cups Homemade Chicken Stock (page 29) or 1/2 chicken stock cube dissolved in the same quantity of boiling water	2 tablespoons cornstarch, mixed with 2 tablespoons water
	2 very fresh free-range eggs, beaten

METHOD

- Clean the lobsters, throwing away the stomach and gills. Chop each into 2-inch pieces with a cleaver.

- Mix the soy sauce, sherry, sugar, salt, and stock and set aside.

- Heat the oil in a wok. When hot, fry the ginger and garlic for 30 seconds, then the black beans, if using, and pork, and fry for another 2 to 3 minutes, or until the pork is no longer pink.

- Add the lobster, heat through, then remove to a warmed dish.

- Add the stock and cornstarch paste to the wok and stir until thick. Add the lobster and heat through.

- Take the wok off the heat and add the raw eggs in a thin stream, stirring until they set in thin threads. If there is not enough heat, return to a gentle heat until they do. Do not overcook.

Stuffed Squid

SERVES 4 TO 6

These days cleaned and frozen squid are frequently available. Squid makes lovely eating as long as it is cooked correctly. Choose small squid, as they will be the most tender.

In Asian kitchens, squid is cooked for no more than a minute or two—just long enough to turn the flesh opaque. Stir-frying is ideal. Alternatively, the bodies make excellent containers for a number of special stuffings. The opening is sewn up with needle and thread or secured with cocktail sticks and the squid is steamed. When cooked, it is sliced into rings and served on a dish—very spectacular.

INGREDIENTS

8 ounces ground pork	1/2 teaspoon sesame oil (optional)
4 tablespoons chopped drained water chestnuts	1 egg
	1 teaspoon salt
1 scallion, washed, trimmed, and finely chopped	1/2 teaspoon ground white pepper
	1 teaspoon cornstarch
2 tablespoons hoisin sauce	4 squid without tentacles, weighing about 1 pound, cleaned and dried
1 garlic clove, crushed	
1 teaspoon *tung choi* (preserved Chinese vegetable), chopped (optional)	

METHOD

■ Mix all the ingredients together in a large bowl and loosely stuff the squid. Don't pack them with too much stuffing or they may burst while cooking.

■ Sew the openings up with a needle and thread or use cocktail sticks to close.

■ Lay the squid in a single layer, and steam them over boiling water for 15 minutes or until they feel tender when prodded with a fork.

■ Remove the threads or cocktail sticks and cut the squid into slices. Lay on a bed of Fried Seaweed (page 47) and serve with dipping sauces such as Tiger Lily's Special Sweet & Sour Sauce (page 26), Vietnamese Dipping Sauce (page 25), or *Nam Prik* (page 24).

■ Any leftover stuffing should be rolled into small balls (use some cornstarch if it feels too sticky), then gently fried in a little oil and served with the squid and dipping sauces.

Stir-Fried Squid with Vegetables

SERVES 6

This is a dish which we predict will quickly become a favorite. The squid is blanched in hot oil for a few seconds only, then stir-fried with the vegetables, to ensure that it remains tender.

INGREDIENTS

2 pounds squid, cleaned, dried, and fancy-cut into 1 1/2-inch squares	4 scallions, washed, trimmed, and chopped
2 tablespoons sherry	1 cup snowpeas, each cut diagonally into 3
2 teaspoons cornstarch	2 teaspoons salt
1 teaspoon freshly grated ginger	1 teaspoon sugar
2 1/2 cups oil, for deep-frying	1/2 teaspoon *Sambol Ulek* (page 25), or 1/2 teaspoon black beans, mashed
4 dried Chinese mushrooms, sliced and soaked	1/2 teaspoon sesame oil

METHOD

■ Put the squid in a bowl with 1 tablespoon of the sherry, the cornstarch and ginger, and leave to marinate for 20 minutes.

■ Heat the cooking oil in a wok, then fry the squid for 30 seconds only in small batches. Be prepared to work quickly—the squid only needs to turn white before being whisked out and dried on paper towels. Keep warm.

■ Carefully pour out all but 2 tablespoons of oil from the wok. Return the wok to the stove and heat until it begins to smoke.

■ Stir-fry the mushrooms and scallions for 1 1/2 minutes.

■ Add the snowpeas, salt, sugar, remaining sherry, and *Sambol Ulek* or black beans. Stir for 1 minute.

■ Finally, add the squid and sesame oil, stir, and serve.

VARIATION

This is a very pretty dish with the white squid contrasting with the black mushrooms and green scallions. If you wish, you can make it look even prettier by sprinkling a pinch of sesame seeds over the top before serving.

133

DECORATIVE SQUID

▪ Squid can be cut in different ways when raw to look decorative. Remember not to slice completely through the skin—only score the top surface about halfway through.

▪ Cut the body vertically, open it out like a book and lay it flat, inner side down. When you have marked out the patterns (see below), cut the squid into squares ready for cooking.

▪ For a diamond cut, use a very sharp vegetable knife and carefully score the skin into diamonds by making long diagonal cuts first in one direction, then the other.

▪ For a porcupine cut, use a pair of kitchen scissors to make random V-shaped snips over the whole surface, all facing the same direction. Very young squid with thin skins are not suitable, as you are likely to cut right through.

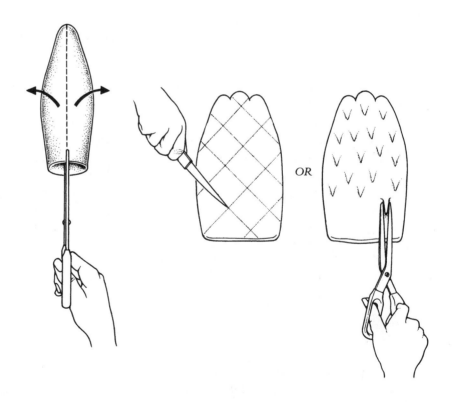

Crab Curry

SERVES 6

Just the words make us drool! Our parents had friends in Sri Lanka called the De Jongs, who owned a pig farm. We, and an odd assortment of friends we knew from embassies abroad, had very memorable parties at their house. A large pig would be spit-roasted over an open pit, and the outside tables would be groaning with dishes of curries, rice, stringhoppers, salads, and breads. We would dance under a velvety black sky, in the light of a huge tropical moon, with lemon-scented flares to keep the mosquitoes at bay.

To drink we were given fresh iced lime or passionfruit juice, or Portello (a dark mixed fruit fizzy drink). The men, especially, downed bottles of *arrack*—a smooth coconut liquor not unlike whiskey, packing a dangerous punch!

After eating the pig and nearly everything else, at about 1 AM, just when we were beginning to wilt, out would come the highlight of the evening— steaming cauldrons of soft-shelled Negombo Lagoon crab curry to eat with *rotis*. Nothing could have tasted as wonderful then or since. This recipe evokes those very happy, very gluttonous memories.

INGREDIENTS

4 to 5 crabs, weighing approximately 3 pounds

1 to 2 teaspoons ground red pepper

2 teaspoons ground coriander

2 teaspoons Roasted Sri Lankan Curry Powder (page 17)

2-inch piece of cinnamon, crushed

2 large onions, chopped and puréed with 3 1/2 cups to 4 1/2 cups water

3 teaspoons salt

1/2 teaspoon dill seeds

2 tablespoons coconut or vegetable oil

6 curry leaves (optional)

1 stalk lemongrass, chopped

2-inch piece *rampe* (pandanus) (optional)

6 onions, sliced

1 teaspoon rice wine vinegar

2 teaspoons ground turmeric

2 limes, seeded and cut into pieces

1/2 cup coconut milk

METHOD

■ Clean each crab, discarding the stomach and gills. Remove the big claws and bash them gently with the back of a knife so the sauce can permeate the meat. Don't be too enthusiastic or you will be picking pieces of shell out of the finished dish! Take off the smaller claws, and reserve. Chop the body into 4 pieces.

■ Dry-roast the red pepper, coriander, curry powder, and crushed cinnamon in a pan for a few minutes, taking care not to burn the mixture. When it begins to darken, add all the remaining ingredients, except the coconut milk, bring to a boil, then gently simmer for 20 minutes.

■ Stir the coconut milk in gently, just before serving. Do not boil, as the curry may curdle.

VARIATIONS

■ Two ingredients which we have not been able to track down in the West are goraka and murunga leaves. Goraka is an orange fruit that turns black when dried in the sun. It is very sour and adds a deep sharp flavor to this and other savory dishes. If you can get it, omit the limes and add 2 pieces goraka, weighing about 4 ounces, instead.

■ Murunga trees are very slim and beautiful. Their feathery leaves resemble mimosa leaves and their fruits are long "drumsticks" which we make into curry. These can be bought in specialty shops. We make murunga leaves into sambols, too. For this recipe, we would add 2 large sprigs of leaves, finely chopped. There is no substitute.

Abalone or Scallops with Chicken & Asparagus

SERVES 6 TO 8

A delicious dish, combining the sweetness and melting tenderness of the abalone with asparagus, the king of vegetables. Scallops, too, are delicious cooked this way. The shortest possible cooking time is needed for these prized shellfish—only until the flesh turns opaque—and don't even think of reheating them.

INGREDIENTS

15-ounce can abalone, drained and rinsed in water or 1 pound scallops	8 ounces chicken breast, finely sliced
	1 tablespoon melted chicken fat or oil
1 pound asparagus spears, lightly steamed, refreshed in cold water, then drained immediately	1 tablespoon sweet sherry or ginger wine
	1/2 teaspoon sugar
1 teaspoon salt	1 1/4 cups Homemade Chicken Stock (page 29) or 1/2 chicken stock cube dissolved in the same quantity of water
3 teaspoons cornstarch	

METHOD

▪ Cut the abalone into thin slices or the scallops into chunks. Each should be a mouthful in size.

▪ Reserve half the asparagus for garnish and chop the rest into 2-inch pieces.

▪ Mix 1/2 teaspoon salt and 1 teaspoon cornstarch together and use to coat the chicken.

▪ Heat the fat or oil in a wok. When smoking, stir-fry the chicken for a few seconds. Add the fish, stir-fry for a few seconds more, then add the asparagus pieces, sherry, sugar, the remaining salt, and the stock.

▪ Mix the remaining cornstarch with 4 tablespoons water to form a cream. Add to the wok and bring to a boil. Stir until the sauce thickens, then place on a serving dish, decorate with the reserved asparagus tips and serve.

VEGETABLES

▲▲▲▲▲▲▲▲▲▲▲▲▲▲▲▲▲

We are very fortunate to have experienced life in the East. We were both born in Bangkok and then moved to Sri Lanka. Sudden violent tropical storms, followed by intense sunshine, would make the earth hiss and steam, encouraging miraculously lush vegetation.

Everything seemed to grow with very little assistance—rubbish dumps would be smothered with tomato, cucumber, melon, pawpaw, and other plants. A papaya (pawpaw) seed planted at the beginning of the year would bear its first luscious fruit within six months and continue to bear fruit more than once a year! Planting a single stalk of lemongrass would result in a small forest within a surprisingly short time.

Chopping down a banana plant, once its comb of bananas was harvested, would encourage new plants to spring up around the original site (bananas grow from rhizomes and can pop up anywhere along the rhizome's length). Even bare sticks pushed into the ground for picket fences would sprout and flower.

Market day was always a treat for us. Grinning toothless old ladies, their gums stained orange by chewing betel (a tobacco-like plant), would walk many miles with huge flat wicker baskets on their heads, bearing a profusion of vegetables and fruit, which could be bought for a few rupees. We loved their fat shiny purple eggplants, the long snake beans and gourds, the red Bombay onions, the chiles of all colors and sizes (the smallest being the deadliest!), and other homegrown produce.

In this book we have tried to select more unusual vegetable (and fruit) recipes for you to try. They are easy to follow—and, as always, you can substitute other vegetables if you wish. You may be enchanted (as we were) to learn that there is one Sri Lankan recipe that involves dipping hibiscus flowers in batter and deep-frying them.

Mallung

DRY GREENS & SPICY COCONUT STIR-FRY

SERVES 4

This is the Asian equivalent of stir-frying and a way of cooking green vegetable leaves so that all the nutrients are preserved. Use cabbage, cauliflower (both the white head and tender leaves surrounding it), spinach or spring greens, or a mixture of all of them. First soak the leaves in salted water to get rid of any insects, rinse thoroughly, then shred very finely with a sharp knife.

Although this is a spicy dish, the flavors are not overpowering, so it would sit quite happily on the table with Western foods.

Leftover *mallung*, when mixed with an equal amount of mashed potato and fried in a little oil like a large pancake, takes good old British bubble and squeak into another dimension.

INGREDIENTS

1 pound shredded greens (8 to 9 cups)	1 teaspoon salt
1/2 teaspoon ground turmeric	1 teaspoon ground red pepper
2 teaspoons ground maldive fish or dried shrimp (optional)	1/2 teaspoon sugar
2 teaspoons lime or lemon juice	3 tablespoons dried coconut

METHOD

■ Put all the ingredients, except the coconut, into a heavy-bottomed frying pan and stir over a moderate heat for 3 to 4 minutes. If the leaves start turning brown, add a tiny amount of water (no more than 2 tablespoons).

■ Add the coconut and stir until the mixture is dry.

■ Serve lukewarm, as a side dish, with rice and curries.

Channa

SERVES 4 TO 6

This is a firm favorite with Chandra's family—she always serves it at family gatherings and none of us has tired of it yet! A deliciously nutty and lightly fragrant dish, it is good with rice or *rotis*. In Sri Lanka it is the equivalent of French fries—served in paper cones on every street corner. Johnnie, Chandra's youngest, is a lover of fast foods, to our disapproval. However, *channa* is also one of his very favorite things—he eats it by the bucketful!

INGREDIENTS

Two 15-ounce cans chickpeas, or 1 1/2 cups dry chickpeas, soaked overnight in 8 cups water

3 tablespoons oil

1 large onion, chopped

1 teaspoon salt

1 teaspoon ground black pepper

2 teaspoons ground cumin

1 teaspoon ground red pepper

1/2 teaspoon ground turmeric

1/2 teaspoon ground coriander

1/4 teaspoon garlic powder

2 tablespoons lemon juice

Chopped coriander leaves (cilantro)

METHOD

■ Drain the canned chickpeas. Or, if using dried chickpeas, rinse them, cover with water, then simmer for 45 minutes, or until tender.

■ Heat the oil in a pan and fry the onion until soft and turning brown.

■ Add the rest of the ingredients (except for the fresh coriander) and stir for about 3 minutes over a medium heat. Take care not to burn—add a little water if necessary.

■ Turn into a bowl, garnish with the chopped coriander, and serve.

VARIATION

Garnish with rings of fresh, thinly sliced onion and tomato; or sprinkle with ground dried maldive fish or shrimp.

Dry Potato & Coconut Curry

SERVES 4

We know we keep saying this is the easiest recipe ever, but do try this one—it must at least be a runner up for the title!

INGREDIENTS

2 large potatoes, weighing approximately 1 pound, washed and dried	1 tablespoon oil
	1 1/4 cups Coconut Sambol (page 30)

METHOD

- Prick the potatoes and either put in a microwave on full power for 3 minutes each or boil in their skins until half-cooked. Do not peel, but cut into chunks about 1 inch in size.

- Heat the oil in a pan, add the potatoes, and fry until just beginning to brown—3 to 5 minutes.

- Add the Coconut Sambol, stir for 1 minute more, and serve.

VARIATION

If a more substantial dish is wanted, add 8 ounces cooked peeled shrimp and a diced green pepper to the potatoes at step 2.

Okra Curry

SERVES 4

Although our tastes in food are similar (we tend to eat anything!), the family is sharply divided over okra (or ladies' fingers). Neither Mum nor Rani can abide its gooey flesh and seeds, while Chandra and Dad simply adore it. As a result, Dad has learned how to cook this Sri Lankan dish but in half the usual quantity.

Okra curry can be made the day before but it does not take kindly to being frozen.

INGREDIENTS

8 ounces okra, washed and dried	3 green chiles, chopped
4 tablespoons oil	3 small onions, chopped
1/2 teaspoon ground turmeric	1 teaspoon ground red pepper
2 teaspoons salt	4 curry leaves (optional)
1 teaspoon each ground cumin and coriander	2-inch piece *rampe* (pandanus, optional)
1 tablespoon ground maldive fish or dried shrimp	3/4 cup coconut milk

METHOD

■ Top and tail the okra. If large, cut into 3 parts; if smaller, cut into 2.

■ Heat the oil in a saucepan, add the okra, turmeric, and salt and stir-fry for about 4 minutes or until the okra turns a light golden brown. Remove with a slotted spoon and set aside.

■ Add all the remaining ingredients, except the coconut milk, to the same oil and fry until brown over a medium heat. Take care that it doesn't burn.

■ Return the fried okra to the pan, add the coconut milk, and simmer gently for about 8 minutes or until a little oil begins to appear on the top of the dish.

■ Serve hot.

143

Gado Gado

INDONESIAN SALAD

SERVES 6 TO 8

With this dish you can really express your artistic soul! Why not decorate with flowers instead of the eggs? The different colors of the ingredients are quite stunning. If you choose to use several smaller plates, they can take the place of traditional floral arrangements on your buffet table. Just take care not to overcook the different vegetables. You may wish to place a small card on the table in front of this dish to explain that the sauce contains peanuts, for anyone who may suffer from an allergic reaction to them.

If making this for a party, it's best to prepare the vegetables the day before and keep them overnight, covered with foil or plastic wrap, in the refrigerator. Quarter the eggs just before serving.

We do not pour the satay sauce over the whole platter, but serve it in bowls alongside. This allows your guests to make their choice of seasoning. Served with a selection of cooked shrimp, chicken breast, sliced meats, *Nam Prik* (page 24), *Sambol Ulek* (page 25), and various chile sauces, this colorful salad will form the main focus of a buffet table.

INGREDIENTS

1/2 small green cabbage	8 ounces tomatoes, cut into quarters (about 2)
8 ounces green beans	
1 large carrot	3 hard-boiled eggs, shelled and quartered, or a selection of edible flowers
2 medium-sized potatoes	
1 cup bean sprouts	1 recipe Satay Sauce (page 28)
1/4 small cucumber, finely sliced or cut into batons	2 scallions, washed, trimmed, and chopped

METHOD

■ Shred the cabbage. Top and tail the beans and break them into 1-inch lengths. Scrape the carrots and cut into sticks similar in size to the beans.

■ Wash the potatoes, cut them into wedges, and boil in their skins for about 4 minutes, or until just cooked.

■ Steam the cabbage, beans, bean sprouts, and carrots separately until each is just cooked, then immediately refresh by putting them in a colander and running cold water over them. The carrots should take no more than 3 minutes, the beans 2 minutes, and the bean sprouts and cabbage only 1 minute. This brief cooking helps retain all the color and flavor. Place the vegetables on a large plate.

■ Add the cucumber to the plate with the quartered tomatoes and eggs, if using, or the flowers.

■ Make up the satay sauce and serve in small bowls, or pour on top of the vegetable platter and sprinkle the chopped scallions over the top.

Pineapple Curry

SERVES 3 TO 4

Pineapples grow like weeds in Sri Lanka and many swear by their apparent slimming properties. Rani once lost nearly 20 pounds in just over eight weeks by eating pineapples every day. Then again, it might have been because the temperature in Sri Lanka at the time was in the high 80s and very humid too.

INGREDIENTS

1 medium-sized fresh pineapple or two 1-pound cans pineapple chunks, drained	1 teaspoon salt
	1 1/2 teaspoons oil
1 1/2 teaspoons ground maldive fish or dried shrimp	1 teaspoon whole mustard seeds
	1 1/2 teaspoons minced onions
1/2 teaspoon ground red pepper	2 green chiles, chopped
1/2 teaspoon ground cinnamon	Grated rind of 1 lemon
1/2 teaspoon ground cumin	1 cup coconut milk
1 teaspoon ground turmeric	

METHOD

- Remove the skin and eyes from the fresh pineapple. Dice the pineapple and mix with all the dry ingredients except the mustard seeds.

- Heat the oil in a saucepan, add the mustard seeds, and stir until they pop.

- Add the onions and fry until they begin to brown.

- Put all the remaining ingredients in the saucepan and simmer gently for 10 to 15 minutes, adding a little extra water if the curry gets too dry. Do not bring to a boil or the coconut milk will curdle.

VARIATION

Add a few curry leaves, a 1-inch piece *rampe* (pandanus), and a little lemongrass to the curry as it simmers.

Cashew Nut Curry

SERVES 3 TO 4

A delightful dish which is full of protein and deliciously meaty. This recipe is a great favorite with vegetarians, and we confess that we do not need meat when this is the main dish. In cashew season in Sri Lanka, the very prettiest girls are seen with great baskets of the nuts by the roadside on the way to Kandy where the University of Peredeniya is situated.

When the Queen visited the University she said it was one of the most beautiful she had ever seen. It is built of pink stone and is surrounded by flowering trees, which rain down a constant shower of pink petals. Our dad's only brother, Professor Gerald Cooray, is a world-famous geologist who lives in Kandy with his wife Joan. For many years he taught at Peredeniya.

The cashew hangs like a pearl from the end of a large fruit, from which an interesting jam and curry is made. As neither the cashew sellers nor their fruit are seen in the West, we will share this recipe with you instead.

INGREDIENTS

8 ounces raw unsalted cashew nuts (about 2 cups)	2 cloves
1 tablespoon oil	3 cardamom pods, crushed
1 medium onion, finely chopped	1 stick of cinnamon
1 1/2 teaspoons ground coriander	1 teaspoon salt
1 teaspoon ground cumin	3/4 cup coconut milk
1/4 teaspoon ground turmeric	1 small green chile, chopped
	4 curry leaves (optional)

METHOD

■ Soak the cashew nuts in water overnight. The next day, rinse and dry the nuts on paper towels.

■ Heat the oil in a pan and fry the onion until soft and beginning to turn brown.

■ Add the rest of the ingredients, bring to a boil, then lower the heat, and simmer for 15 minutes.

Mixed Vegetable Stir-Fry

SERVES 4 TO 6

Everyone has a special vegetable stir-fry recipe. This is one of our favorites because of the contrasts in color and texture. But feel free to add your own ingredients—and never be afraid to experiment.

When we first started selling our products at yard sales, and then at trade fairs, we lost count of the number of inquiries from people who were afraid of experimenting. If we suggested spreading a teaspoon of one of our relishes over a lamb chop and then grilling it, we were invariably asked if it would be all right to put it on a pork chop or even a chicken roast. We would say "Put it on your old man's socks if you think he'll eat it!" Many think that Asian cooking is more difficult than it really is.

INGREDIENTS

4 ounces *pak choi* (Chinese cabbage) or spinach (about 2 1/4 cups)	1 garlic clove, crushed
1/2 cup whole baby corn	1 thin ginger slice, crushed
1/2 cup broccoli florets	1 tablespoon soy sauce
1/2 cup snowpeas	1 teaspoon salt
1/2 cup button mushrooms	1/2 teaspoon sugar
1/2 cup canned water chestnuts	1 teaspoon cornstarch, mixed with 1 tablespoon sherry
1/2 cup bamboo shoots	1 teaspoon sesame oil (optional)
2 teaspoons vegetable oil	

METHOD

■ Wash all the vegetables. Cut the cabbage or spinach into strips. Leave the corn whole if it is very small (about the size of a baby's finger) or cut into 2 if any bigger. Break the broccoli into small florets, and cut the mushrooms and water chestnuts in half. Slice the bamboo shoots into strips.

■ Put the cabbage, corn, broccoli, and snowpeas into a pan of boiling water, cook for no more than 1 minute, then strain in a colander and place under cold running water to refresh.

■ Heat a large wok, add the vegetable oil and, when hot, add the garlic and ginger and swirl them around. Add all the vegetables and stir-fry for 2 minutes only.

■ Add the soy sauce, salt, sugar, and the cornstarch and sherry mixture. Stir to thicken, add the sesame oil, and serve immediately.

Stir-Fried Beans

SERVES 4 TO 6

This is another of our favorite vegetable recipes. Use either French beans (*haricot verts*) or runner beans. Just be sure that they are at their youngest and snappiest best. No stringy old has-beans (excuse the pun!) for this dish, please.

INGREDIENTS

1 tablespoon oil	1 pound fresh green beans, washed, trimmed, and cut into short lengths
1 garlic clove, crushed	1 tablespoon soy sauce
1 thin ginger slice, shredded	1 teaspoon sugar
2 ounces pancetta, cut into small strips	1 teaspoon salt

METHOD

▪ Heat a wok, add the oil, and swirl it around. Put the garlic, ginger, and pancetta in the wok and stir-fry for 1 minute.

▪ Add the beans, and the remaining ingredients, with 1 teaspoon water, and stir-fry for another 3 minutes.

VARIATIONS

▪ Vegetarians can leave out the pancetta.

▪ Add a splash of fish sauce and a small chopped chile at the end, to give this dish more Thai flavor.

149

Stir-Fried Chinese Cabbage with Shrimp

SERVES 4 TO 6

INGREDIENTS

1 small green cabbage or *pak choi*, weighing approximately 1 pound	1 teaspoon ginger wine or sweet sherry (optional)
2 tablespoons oil	1 teaspoon cornstarch, mixed with 1 table-spoon water
2 scallions, washed, trimmed, and chopped	2 ounces cooked shrimp (about 1/2 cup)
2 tablespoons soy sauce	Salt and pepper (optional)
1 teaspoon sugar	

METHOD

■ Wash the cabbage or *pak choi*, then shred finely with a sharp knife.

■ Heat a wok and add the oil. When smoking, add the cabbage and stir-fry for 3 minutes.

■ Add the rest of the ingredients and stir-fry until the shrimp are warmed through and the sauce thickens. Taste and add extra salt and pepper if necessary.

VARIATIONS

■ Vegetarians can omit the shrimp, and substitute 1/2 cup sliced mushrooms instead.

■ If you wish, sprinkle a little ground dried shrimp over this dish when serving, to further deepen the taste of the fresh shrimp.

Bean Sprouts

Bean Sprouts are everyone's favorite, especially our mother's. She goes wild for the larger, firmer soy bean sprouts which are available from Chinese specialty stores. Sprouts are very nutritious and raw bean sprouts are delicious added to green salads, giving a satisfying crunch to every mouthful. Although bean sprouts are available from most supermarkets, they are very easy to grow. Try harvesting your own soybean or mung bean (the smaller, more familiar) sprouts. Seeds are readily available from health food stores. Just gather the following items:

INGREDIENTS

2 tablespoons or 2 ounces mung or soy beans	A small piece of cheesecloth to cover the mouth of the jar
1 large glass jar	1 large rubber band to go around the neck of the jar

METHOD

▪ Wash the beans thoroughly in plenty of clean water. Put them into the jar and secure the cloth with a rubber band around the rim.

▪ Place the jar on its side on a tray and put in a dark warm place.

▪ Take the jar out twice a day and rinse with water. The seeds should be fully sprouted within four days or so. Do not let them grown green leaves, as these make the sprouts bitter.

▪ Wash very well in fresh water, then top and tail them when ready for use.

Quick-Fried Bean Sprouts

SERVES 4 TO 6

INGREDIENTS

1 tablespoon oil	1/2 teaspoon salt
3 scallions, washed, trimmed, and chopped	1/2 teaspoon garlic salt
1 pound bean sprouts	Pinch of sugar
1 1/2 teaspoons cornstarch	
3 tablespoons Homemade Chicken Stock (page 29) or use 1/8 chicken stock cube dissolved in 2 tablespoons boiling water	

METHOD

■ Heat a wok and add the oil. When it begins to smoke, throw in the scallions and stir-fry for 30 seconds.

■ Add the bean sprouts and fry until they become translucent.

■ Mix the cornstarch with the stock and add to the pan, together with the salt, garlic salt, and sugar.

■ Heat through for another minute, and serve.

VARIATION

As always, you can add what you like to this recipe—any sliced meats, and extra vegetables like shredded cabbage, grated carrot, mushrooms, or bamboo shoots. Just remember that bean sprouts are mainly water and only need the minimum of cooking time. Cook whatever ingredients you use in sequence, according to how long they need to cook. For instance, meat or fibrous vegetables should be stir-fried after the scallions but well before the bean sprouts.

SWEETS

▲▲▲▲▲▲▲▲▲▲▲▲▲▲▲▲▲

Asian meals do not end traditionally with a sweet, as in the West. As we have our choice of delicious fruits, we tend to choose them instead. We used to enjoy sweet treats during the day, or for tiffin at 3 PM when everything really did stop for tea. Sri Lankan confections are quite heavy going—usually stodgy, very sweet, and deep-fried in coconut oil. Thula balls, for instance, are made by kneading together jaggery (palm sugar) and sesame seeds until the mixture sticks together and then forming them into balls.

Delicious Muscat is offered to guests who always feel free to pop in. (One thing we at first found strange in the West was the odd practice of waiting to be formally invited.) We also used to enjoy eating curds—very thick, acidic buffalo or cow's milk yogurt sold in round clay pots by the roadside—mixed with jaggery or freshly harvested honey.

We have included our favorite family recipes in this chapter. Many are inspired by sweets we have tasted in the past, but some are treats we invented ourselves to keep our own kids happy when they were small. Those who are young at heart will, we hope, relish them as much.

Turtle "Eggs"

SERVES 4 TO 6

Rani took Dad to Singapore and Malaysia in the late eighties. Disoriented from jet lag, Dad slipped in the bathroom on the first night and had to be admitted to a hospital for a week with severe concussion. Although very frail, after he was discharged, he insisted we all resume our journey to the east coast to see the gigantic leatherback turtles lay their eggs.

Because of intense tourist interest, the turtle numbers had been dwindling, as the reptiles sought quieter beaches to lay their eggs. The manager of our resort warned us not to be disappointed if we did not see any—they tended to come to lay in the early hours of the morning and they went to remote parts of the beach. There was no way we could get Dad, who was still very shaky, to these far-off beaches, and he could not be left on his own.

On the second morning at 9 AM, in broad daylight, a huge turtle hauled her way out of the water, tears streaming down her face, and laid a clutch of eggs directly in front of Dad's beach hut. It was magical and inexplicable and the manager took photographs of all of us with the turtle for visitor postcards.

These sweet rice dumplings look like turtle eggs. They are as smooth and waxy in appearance, though many times smaller of course. They make a refreshing ending to a meal consisting of a number of rich, savory main dishes.

INGREDIENTS

4 ounces glutinous rice powder (get it from a Chinese food supplier—there is no substitute)

1 tablespoon sugar

1 teaspoon almond extract

2 1/4 cups whole milk

METHOD

■ Mix the rice powder with 1 teaspoon of the sugar and 2 tablespoons water to form a soft but stiff dough. Add more water if the mixture seems too stiff. Break off tiny amounts, about the size of a marble, and roll into rounds.

■ Put the rest of the sugar, almond extract, and milk into a pan and bring it almost to a boil. Watch that it doesn't boil over!

■ Drop in the "eggs" and simmer for about 3 minutes. They will rise to the surface when cooked.

■ Turtle eggs are delicious served hot or chilled. Add a few crushed ice cubes if they are served cold.

Muscat

Muscat is somewhat similar to very fragrant Turkish delight, but we believe it is far superior. Serve it in very small quantities, as it is so rich.

Our paternal grandfather's brother, Johnnie Cooray, was married to a very sweet lady called Jessie. She spoke no English, only Singhalese which we could not understand, but she was very fond of us. We always pestered Mum and Dad to make a detour after church to stop by their house. When we did, Aunty Jessie would give us lots of kisses and cuddles and, of course, mountains of homemade sweets, particularly muscat, as she knew we loved it so much.

We would like to dedicate this recipe to the Sri Lankan cricket team of 1996, who won the World Cup against all odds. The sheer exuberance and fine effort of this young team, against the sad background of terrorist activity in Sri Lanka, certainly helped give our people something to dance about in the streets! The Sri Lankan flag is a lion proudly holding a sword. The predominant colors are green, yellow, and orange, and we like to color our muscat accordingly (see Variation below).

INGREDIENTS

3 cups flour	Seeds from 3 cardamom pods, crushed
6 cups white sugar	1/2 cup rosewater
1 1/4 cups whole milk	8 ounces ghee, melted (1 cup)
1/2 cup raw unsalted cashew nuts, cut into slivers	

METHOD

■ Mix the flour with a little water and form into a ball. Tie in a clean kitchen towel.

■ Put into a bowl and add 4 1/2 cups water.

■ Swish the ball in the water and keep it moving until all the starch comes out. Do this at least 4 to 5 times, until you are left with just a sticky ball of gluten in the kitchen towel. Discard this residue.

■ Put the starch water and sugar in a heavy-bottomed saucepan. Bring to a boil, reduce the heat and keep stirring.

- After about 45 minutes the mixture should become very thick. Add the milk, cashews, crushed cardamom, and rosewater. Then add the ghee, spoonful by spoonful. When it turns thick and transparent, take off the heat.

- Spread onto a well-buttered tray, and leave to set at room temperature.

- Cut into small chunks and eat with bliss!

VARIATION

To replicate the 3 colors of the Sri Lankan flag, omit the rosewater at step 5. When the mixture turns thick and transparent, take off the heat and divide into 3 equal portions. Color and flavor 1 portion with 1 teaspoon vanilla extract and a few drops of yellow food coloring, 1 portion with 1 teaspoon pistachio extract and a few drops of green coloring, and the last portion with 1 teaspoon orange flower water or orange extract and a few drops of orange coloring.

Vattalapan

SERVES 6 TO 8

Many Sri Lankan desserts are very oily and heavy, made with coconut and rice flour and deep-fried in coconut oil. Heart attack material! *Vattalapan* is an exception—a dark, deliciously aromatic custard made with coconut milk and palm sugar and flavored with cardamom and rosewater. Serve in small portions to begin with—rest assured your guests will come back for seconds or even thirds!

INGREDIENTS

3/4 cup jaggery (palm sugar) or dark brown sugar

2 1/2 cups coconut milk

6 eggs

1/2 teaspoon ground cardamom

1/2 teaspoon ground mixed spice or allspice

3 teaspoons rosewater

12 raw unsalted cashew nuts, halved

METHOD

■ Heat the sugar and coconut milk in a saucepan to dissolve gently.

■ Beat the rest of the ingredients, except the cashew nuts, together until frothy, then add to the coconut milk mixture.

■ Pour into a 1-quart well-buttered container or 6 to 8 well-buttered individual heatproof dishes and steam until the custard sets.

■ Decorate with the cashew nuts and serve cold.

Almond Tea

SERVES 4 TO 6

Although very simple to prepare, this sweet is so pretty and refreshing to the palate that our recipe has gone around the world many times, having been so much requested by friends and family. The small opaque diamonds of almond cream float in crystal-clear, sweetened ice water. It's very pretty served in a hollowed-out watermelon or ice bowl (pages 160–161).

INGREDIENTS

1/2 cup sugar	2 (15-ounce) cans evaporated milk
Two 1-ounce packets unflavored gelatin	1/2 teaspoon almond extract

METHOD

■ Heat 1/4 cup sugar with 1 cup water to make a syrup. Then cool and refrigerate.

■ Heat the remaining 1/4 cup sugar and 1 cup water in a pan to dissolve.

■ Sprinkle the gelatin on top and warm in a saucepan until the gelatin dissolves.

■ Mix in the evaporated milk and almond extract, then pour into a large shallow baking tray (rinsed in water). Refrigerate until set.

■ Cut into diamond shapes, then serve with the ice cold syrup in a pretty glass bowl. Float a few rose petals on top.

Steamed Butter Cake

SERVES 4 TO 6   **O**n a quick stroll around any of Chinatown's bakeries, you will always see a display of large fluffy golden slabs of this cake. Unlike Western cakes, which are baked, this one is steamed, which gives it an interesting texture and lightness. Serve it in chunks, with whipped creamed flavored with a little ginger wine and sliced crystallized ginger.

INGREDIENTS

2 large eggs	6 tablespoons butter, melted then cooled
1/2 teaspoon salt	6 tablespoons half-and-half
1/2 cup sugar	1 1/2 cups self-rising flour, sifted with 1/2 teaspoon baking powder

METHOD

▪ Separate the eggs and whisk the whites with the salt in a clean bowl until stiff. Add the sugar, a bit at a time, and whisk again until it stands in peaks.

▪ Add the egg yolks, whisk again, then lightly mix in the butter and half-and-half.

▪ Use a rubber spatula to fold in the flour. Try to keep the mixture as fluffy and light as possible.

▪ Cut some greaseproof paper to the size of a 7-inch steamer with a 4-inch overlap, and butter lightly. Gently pour the mixture into the steamer, cover, and steam for 20 minutes over boiling water.

▪ Turn the cake out, cut into slabs, and serve immediately.

VARIATIONS

▪ Another way of serving this cake is with a mango coulis or purée (take 2 very ripe mangoes and pass the flesh through a sieve or food mill, with 1 tablespoon pure orange juice).

▪ Or serve it with Coconut Ice Cream (page 160).

Coconut Ice Cream & Mango Flowers

SERVES 6 TO 8

Chandra's daughter, Neisha, was a very fussy eater when small, and seemed to survive on no more than a packet of twiglets a day. Even getting her to drink her milk as a baby was a major performance—one of us would have to carry her and dance around the room while Mother sang strange high-pitched songs from Chinese operas. If the baby approved she would design to swallow one minute mouthful. If not, the whole palaver would start again until we were all exhausted.

Thank goodness Neisha grew out of her picky eating habits. She is now the family's official cake-maker and producer of desserts for parties. This is one of her favorite recipes and she makes the most beautiful ice bowls using not only flowers, but herbs and fruit, too.

INGREDIENTS

1 3/4-pint tub of the best-quality full cream vanilla ice cream (or make your own)

2 1/2 cups coconut milk

Grated rind and juice of 1 lime

2 mangoes (ripe but still fairly hard)

METHOD

- Soften the ice cream, fold in the rest of the ingredients, except the mangoes, and put back into the freezer to harden.

- Scoop the ice cream into small bowls and serve in an ice bowl (see below).

- Peel the mangoes. Then, using a knife, carefully cut segments lengthwise to resemble flower petals. Use to decorate the coconut ice cream.

MAKING A DECORATIVE ICE BOWL

You will need:

INGREDIENTS

a handful of edible flowers

a selection of sliced fresh fruit with the skin on (e.g., oranges, lemons, and kiwi fruit) or small whole fruit (e.g., kumquats or green and black grapes)

2 metal or plastic bowls of different circumferences, one smaller by at least 1 inch diameter than the other

METHOD

■ The smaller your inner bowl, the thicker the sides of your ice bowl and the longer it will take to melt. It defeats the purpose to have the bowl too thick and ungainly, so experiment with plain water until you are happy with the result. Quarter fill the larger bowl with water and add a few flowers or slices of fruit.

■ Place the other bowl in this bowl, put a small cup or some other heavy object in it to weigh it down, then put the bowls in the freezer to set, making sure they are level. The water should only come about halfway up the outside of the smaller bowl.

■ Take the bowls out, add more water and flowers, and refreeze.

■ When ready to serve, take the bowls out, remove the weight from the smaller bowl and pour a little hot water into it.

■ Give the bowls a twist in the opposite directions and remove the smaller bowl. Your ice bowl, complete with edible decoration, is now ready to be filled with a number of iced desserts, such as sorbets, melon balls, or fruit salads.

■ Ice bowls only last for 2 hours or so in a warm room or in summer, so fill at the last possible moment, on the point of service. And, of course, you will remember to put your ice bowl on a serving dish which is deep enough to catch drips or (like one of us) you will find your buffet table very damp indeed!

VARIATIONS

■ Add a few drops of food coloring to the water. Those who really have time can express their artistic leanings by using several different colors, adding only a little water at a time and tilting the bowl carefully between each filling and freezing. You will end up with a very beautiful rainbow-colored container, but this is so fiddly and time-consuming we only recommend it for very special occasions.

■ Using soda water will ensure that your ice bowl is crystal clear.

Marshmallows

One of our funniest memories was helping our cousin Pauline Smith to make a gigantic trayful of marshmallows for her parents' Silver Wedding Anniversary party. The only place to put it was on top of our refrigerator; but in our haste, we forgot to cover the tray with a clean kitchen towel. When we went to see if the marshmallows were ready, we found that a little transparent lizard or gecko had fallen into the nearly set mixture. Determined to escape, it was executing perfect breast strokes, worthy of an Olympic gold medalist, but in extremely slow motion. Of course, we had to start again!

INGREDIENTS

1-ounce packet unflavored gelatin	1 1/3 cups confectioners' sugar, sifted
1 1/2 cups white granulated sugar	Food coloring (see below)

METHOD

■ Put 1/4 cup water in a bowl and sprinkle the gelatin on top. Leave for 10 minute to get spongy.

■ Pour another 1/4 cup water into a saucepan, add the granulated sugar, and bring to a boil. Reduce the heat, add the gelatin mixture, and keep stirring over a low heat until the gelatin has dissolved and the mixture becomes syrupy.

■ Remove from the heat and leave to cool down slightly, then pour into a very large heatproof mixing bowl, and beat with an electric whisk until very light, thick, and foamy.

■ Divide into separate bowls and color/flavor with any of the following combinations. For pink, use 1/2 teaspoon raspberry or rose flavoring and a drop of red coloring, if needed. For green, use 1/2 teaspoon pistachio and a drop of green coloring. For yellow, use 1/2 teaspoon pineapple extract and a drop of yellow coloring. For white, use 1/2 teaspoon vanilla extract. Marshmallows are far more appetizing when delicately presented, so go easy on the colors and flavorings.

■ Turn the mixture into lightly oiled flat baking trays and leave to set (about 9 hours or overnight) in a cool place or in the refrigerator. When set, cut into cubes or diamonds and dust with the sifted confectioners' sugar.

■ Stored in an airtight container, the marshmallows will last for at least a week.

Peking Dust

—— PURÉED CHESTNUTS COVERED IN WHIPPED CREAM ——

SERVES 4 TO 6

This dish is in memory of our maternal grandfather whom we never knew. A Manchurian warlord, he brought his five wives (our grandmother and four concubines) and 22 children to live within the gates of the Forbidden City. Do you wonder that the whole family was enraptured by the film *The Last Emperor*? Mum remembered well the hot, dusty streets of Peking in summer.

Peking Dust can be made up to 3 hours before serving.

INGREDIENTS

1 1/2 pounds raw chestnuts or 1 pound chestnut purée

3/4 cup confectioners' sugar, or 2 1/2 tablespoons confectioners' sugar if using sweetened purée

1 1/4 cups heavy cream

1 tablespoon confectioners' sugar, to dust the top of the dessert

METHOD

- Cut a small cross in each chestnut and either roast or boil them until soft.

- Peel them while still hot, then push through a strainer or put in a food processor on high until almost reduced to a powder.

- Add 10 tablespoons of the confectioners' sugar, then heap on a pretty plate in the form of a mountain. If using sweetened purée, omit the sugar and go straight to this stage. Taste and add more sugar if necessary.

- Whisk the cream to soft peak stage with the rest of the sugar and carefully cover the chestnut mountain, using a knife to smooth the sides.

- Use a fine-mesh strainer to sift a little confectioners' sugar over the cream, before serving.

VARIATION

Those who like to give their desserts a little extra pizzazz can stir 1 to 2 teaspoons kirsch (cherry liqueur) or other spirit into the cream after whisking it at step 4.

Avocado Ice Cream

SERVES 4

Avocados grow to an immense size—larger than grapefruit—in the East, and are more round than pear-shaped. Their flesh is also much creamier and softer. You may only be used to eating them as savories, in salads or stuffed with shrimp, but we prefer to eat them sweetened any day.

Because of the general liking for condensed milk in tea and coffee (we warned you of the prevalent sweet tooth here!), we would always have a can of the gooey stuff in the refrigerator. Chandra would mix avocado with condensed milk and powdered milk to make a thick purée and we would sit in the branches of our guava tree scoffing bowlfuls. No wonder we were so plump as children!

This dish is not strictly ice cream—more like a rich Indian *kulfi*. As with most of the recipes in this chapter, serve in small quantities!

INGREDIENTS

10 tablespoons clotted or heavy cream	2 large ripe avocados, weighing about 1 1/2 pounds
1 tablespoon sugar	

METHOD

■ Whip the cream, fold in the sugar, and set aside.

■ Cut the avocados in half and scoop out the soft flesh. Be sure to scrape out every bit of the dark green flesh nearest the skin—it gives the deepest color. Mash with a fork, then mix into the cream mixture. Cover and freeze until almost set.

■ Take out of the freezer and put in a food processor on high for a few minutes until all the ice particles have broken down.

■ Cover and return to the freezer until hard.

■ Scoop into small balls and serve with a sharp fruit sauce (see below) or very thin, crisp, sweet butter cookies.

VARIATIONS

■ You can make this dessert a little less rich by stirring in the juice of 2 limes at the point of freezing.

■ To make a sharp fruit sauce to serve with the ice cream, purée 1/2 pound raspberries, strawberries, or black currants with the juice of 1/2 a lime and put through a strainer. Add a little sugar to taste.

■ We remember going to relations' house and being served this recipe in its unfrozen state. It tasted divine and would sometimes be delicately flavored with crushed cardamom seeds. Cover with plastic wrap or lay a damp piece of parchment paper over the surface to exclude the air, and don't prepare too long in advance or it will oxidize and start to turn black.

Batatada

—— PORTUGUESE POTATO CAKE ——

MAKES A 7-INCH CAKE

Rani's friend and colleague Larry O'Neil has almost as mixed a background as we do! His mother is Spanish/Filipina and this is one of her own handed-down-the-generations recipes. Batatada barely rises and is a heavy solid cake, but it is very delicious and has a lovely pale golden color. It is found in many Southeast Asian countries in various forms, thanks to the seafaring Dutch and Portuguese.

Larry says this is an office favorite and he makes it in at least double the quantity given in the recipe.

INGREDIENTS

1 1/2 pounds potatoes, peeled and boiled	1 cup self-rising flour
2 whole eggs	1 1/4 cups dried coconut
2 extra egg yolks	1 cup superfine sugar
1 cup butter, softened	

METHOD

■ Preheat the oven to 350° F., and grease a 7-inch cake pan.

■ Put all the ingredients into a blender and blend well.

■ Turn into the buttered pan and bake until a skewer plunged into the middle comes out clean (1 to 1 1/2 hours).

■ Cut into small slices and serve warm or cold with whipped cream if desired.

VARIATION

Add either 1 to 2 ripe mashed bananas or 3 tablespoons crushed pineapple pieces or 1 teaspoon vanilla extract or rosewater to the above recipe at step 2.

GLOSSARY

Agar-Agar—The vegetarian alternative to gelatin, agar-agar is made from various kinds of seaweed. Dishes made with agar-agar possess a unique crunchy texture and will set at room temperature, an added advantage in the East where many households still do not possess refrigeration.

Allspice—Also known as Jamaican pepper, this fragrant berry combines the flavors of cinnamon, nutmeg, and cloves in one spice. Equally good in savory or sweet dishes.

Bamboo Shoots—Bland in taste, like bean curd, bamboo shoots have the chameleon-like ability to absorb seasonings, and will add a delicious crunch to stir-fried and braised dishes. Widely available in canned form, they should be drained before use.

Bean Curd/Tofu—Made from puréed yellow soy beans, tofu is essentially tasteless, but possesses high protein value. It is sold in the form of white gelatinous cakes covered in water, and can be added to meat, fish, or vegetables where it will absorb all the flavors of the dish. It can also be coated in rice flour or cornstarch, fried and added to other dishes or it can be eaten by itself with dipping sauces.

Bean Sprouts—These are the shoots of sprouted mung beans or soy beans. If stir-frying bean sprouts, cook for no more than a couple of minutes to retain their crispness. They also make a welcome addition to salads.

Besan/Chickpea flour—Especially good as a batter for coating deep-fried foods, as it sticks like glue.

Bhajii—A popular snack made from spicy onions coated in chickpea flour batter and then deep-fried.

Blachan/Shrimp Paste—Often used to give the familiar fish undertone to Thai dishes, this paste is made of dried shrimp and possesses a very strong odor. If the paste is wrapped in aluminum foil and grilled or baked in the oven for approximately 10 minutes, it will blend more easily with other ingredients. Use sparingly.

Black Beans—Salted soy beans commonly used to add a distinctive flavor to Chinese dishes. Should be soaked for 10 minutes before use to remove excess salt, then mashed to release the maximum flavor.

Bok Choy—A type of Chinese cabbage that is freely available for sale in Chinese super-markets and easily grown at home from seeds, as long as it is well watered. The delicate flavor of this long green leaf, with its white central stalk, enhances many recipes and requires a minimum of cooking. Chinese greens (e.g., *choi sam*) and Chinese cabbage are also sometimes known as *pak choi*.

Cardamom—These fragrant little black seeds are encased in small green, white, or black pods. They can be used whole or the seeds can be extracted from the pods before cooking. They are often used to add depth to curries and braised dishes. Also frequently used in cakes and sweets in the East or as a breath-freshener. We refer throughout the book to green cardamom pods.

Chiles—A common ingredient in Sri Lankan, Indian, and Thai cuisine, chiles come in a variety of colors and shapes, fresh and dried, pieces and powdered. The general rule is that the smaller the chile, the hotter the taste! The heat is provided by the seeds in the chile pod and these can be removed from fresh chiles if a milder taste is required.

Cinnamon—The bark of the cinnamon tree produces this fragrant spice, which is used equally in savory and sweet dishes in the East.

Cloves—The pungent aromatic dried bud of a tropical tree, only a small number is required to add a subtle tone to savory or sweet dishes.

Coconut Milk/Cream—The flesh of the coconut is grated and mixed with a very small amount of warm water to obtain the thick milk known as coconut cream. The same pulp can then be squeezed again, twice more, to make a thinner liquid known as coconut milk. Coconut milk is widely available ready-to-use in cans. Dried coconut is well known to Western cooks, usually for cake-making.

Coriander—The main spice in most curries when mixed with cumin and turmeric. Also known as *dhania*, coriander can be found as seeds, powder, or as fresh leaves. The seeds can be used whole or ground. A stronger flavor is gained by dry-roasting them for 2 to 3 minutes over a medium heat in a heavy-bottomed pan until they darken in color. The fresh leaves are also known as cilantro or Chinese parsley. The leaves should be kept refrigerated in a plastic bag and are easily grown at home from coriander seeds. Substituting dried coriander for fresh will not give the same flavor; ordinary parsley should be used in recipes if fresh cilantro or coriander cannot be obtained.

Cumin—Cumin seeds can be used whole, ground, or roasted in the same way as coriander seeds. Sometimes roasted ground cumin is sprinkled on top of cooked dishes as a final flavoring.

Curry Leaves—Also known as *karapincha* in Sri Lanka, curry leaves are an important element in Asian cooking. A few leaves added to any dish will impart a delicate curry smell and flavor. The leaves can be fried and crumbled into dishes for a more robust taste. There is no alternative.

Dhal—Lentils cooked with spices and served with rice or breads. A nourishing vegetarian alternative to meat.

Dosa/Thosai—Rice, lentil flour, and spices made into a thin, delicious, savory pancake.

Fennel—The flavoring agent used in licorice. Extremely good with meat dishes to impart a sweet, fragrant flavor.

Fenugreek—These yellow seeds are used primarily to accentuate the flavor of lighter spices. Particularly good with vegetables, the seeds are slightly bitter and should be used sparingly.

Fish Sauce—Also known as *nam pla* in Thailand. Made from pressed salted anchovies, this thin brown liquid is often used instead of salt in Thai cuisine.

Five Spice Powder—A mixture of five spices, ground to a powder, commonly used in Chinese cooking. Consists of star anise, fennel seeds, cinnamon, Szechuan pepper, and cloves. The pretty, flower-like star anise provides the distinctive aniseed smell and flavor of this mixture.

Galangal—A member of the ginger family, galangal is used extensively in Southeast Asian cooking. Pound in a mortar and pestle or process in a blender with a little water. The dried form of galangal requires soaking before it can be treated as above.

Garlic—Along with ginger and onions, garlic forms the "trinity" required for most Asian cuisines. The medicinal properties of garlic are now well known and fresh garlic, dried garlic flakes, and powdered garlic are widely available.

Ghee—Clarified butter used for cooking foods at high temperatures where ordinary butter would burn. Easily made by melting butter and separated the clear clarified butter from the residue.

Ginger—This aromatic root provides a warm, spicy note in savory or sweet dishes. Fresh ginger should be peeled and grated or crushed, or puréed with a little water in a blender or food processor, before use. Can also be found in dried powder form, although this is not in the same class as fresh ginger. Ginger can be stored in the refrigerator, wrapped in plastic wrap, or buried in sandy soil, where it will not only retain its freshness but will produce more shoots for use, if it is watered sparingly.

Hodi—A versatile Sri Lankan coconut soup customarily used to moisten Stringhoppers (see page 86) or as the basis of white vegetable curries.

Hoisin Sauce—A thick sweetish brown sauce made of soy beans, garlic, chiles, and spices—especially good for flavoring barbecues and grills.

Hoppers—also known as *appa* in Sri Lanka, hoppers are a cross between a pancake and a crumpet. Made by swishing a rice flour batter into a small rounded pan (similar to a *karahi* used in Balti cooking), covering the pan with a lid and baking it, the edges of the hopper turn crispy brown while the center becomes light and spongy. Often eaten in Sri Lanka for breakfast with an egg cooked in the center.

Jaggery—Brown sugar made from palms. Used commonly in Sri Lanka in place of cane sugar and, mixed with coconut, it is the basis of many Sri Lankan desserts and sweets.

Kaffir Lime Leaves—Often used in Thai dishes, these leaves add the distinctive aroma of limes. If unavailable, grated lime rind may be substituted.

Lemongrass—A grasslike plant which imparts a delicate citrus flavor. Extensively used in Thai and Sri Lankan cuisine. Grated lemon rind can be substituted, but will have a stronger flavor.

Lentils—Also known as *dhal*, these are packed with protein and are the staple food of many households in the East. There are many different types of lentils, the commonest being: *moong dhal* (the green whole grain is the mung bean used for bean sprouts, while the yellow type is hulled and split); *urid dhal* (black is the whole grain; white is split and hulled); and *channa dhal* (a branch of the split pea family and considerably larger than *moong dhal*). It is believed that the addition of asafoetida when cooking lentils reduces the unfortunate side effect of eating too many beans—flatulence!

Maldive Fish—An essential ingredient of many Sri Lankan dishes, maldive fish is indigenous to the Maldive Islands, after which it is named. Flakes of this dried fish are used, like fish sauce in Thailand, to add a light fishy undertone to many dishes. If unavailable, ground dried shrimp are an acceptable alternative.

Mushrooms—The Chinese use a wide variety of mushrooms in cooking, from button mushrooms to wood ear and straw mushrooms. Wood ears are a dried fungus and should be soaked for 20 minutes in water, drained, rinsed, and have their stems removed before being sliced and cooked. Straw mushrooms are usually sold in cans and should be drained before use. They have a special affinity with crab dishes. Both these mushrooms are used to add texture rather than taste, as they are quite bland in flavor.

Mustard Seeds—Commonly found as black or yellow seeds, these seeds are used to add pungency to many Asian dishes. They can be used whole or ground in a mortar and pestle or a coffee grinder.

Nutmeg—Although usually sold in powdered form, fresh nutmeg is preferred, stored in an airtight jar, and grated as required. The outer covering of the nutmeg is known as mace and this is exceptionally good in green vegetable dishes.

Oil—The best types of oils to use when cooking Asian food are those that are not too highly flavored, such as vegetable, sunflower, and corn oil. Olive oil is never used in authentic Asian dishes, as it is too strongly flavored and is an uncommon ingredient in the East.

Oyster Sauce—A thick brown sauce made from oyster extract, sugar, soy sauce, and spices, often used in Chinese cooking. Flavors vegetables particularly well.

Pakora—Small vegetable or meat pieces dipped in chickpea flour batter before being deep-fried.

Pandanus Leaves—Also known as *rampe* in Sri Lanka and used in all sorts of dishes, from biriyanis to curries.

Sesame Seeds—The seeds of this annual herbaceous tropical plant are used in both savory and sweet dishes. The seeds can be roasted in a dry nonstick pan (for only a few seconds, as they burn in the wink of an eye) for a stronger flavor. Sesame oil is used for flavoring cooked dishes but rarely used undiluted for cooking, as it too burns very easily.

Sherry—Dry sherry is an acceptable substitute for dishes requiring rice wine, although we tend to use sweet sherry more often.

Soy Sauce—An essential ingredient in Chinese cuisine, soy sauce comes in a light or dark variety. The light soy sauce is more commonly used in stir-frying, while the dark variety is used to impart a richer flavor to braised and slow-cooked dishes.

Stringhoppers—The Sri Lankan name for this specialty is *idi-appung*. Made from steamed or roasted rice flour, which is then laboriously squeezed through a mold with tiny holes, the result is thin rice noodles.

Tamarind—A velvety fruit pod, the liquid from the pulp is used to add a distinctive sweet/sour note to dishes. Most commonly found in dried block form, the juice can be extracted by soaking a 2-inch piece in enough hot water to cover, leaving it for 30 minutes, then squeezing the pulp and straining the liquid before use. The residue of seeds and pulp is discarded.

Tung Choi—This is Chinese preserved cabbage and garlic shoots, known by a variety of names—Tianjin preserved vegetable (made from Tianjin cabbage), winter cabbage pickle, or *tung tsai*. These savory, salty, brownish flakes of preserved vegetable are usually sold in sachets or lovely little earthenware pottery jars. An invaluable addition to the pantry, *tung choi* can be used to give additional flavor to soups, fried rice, noodles, meat, or bland vegetable dishes.

Turmeric—The poor man's saffron, this hard yellow root gives a golden hue to dishes when used in powder form. Careful handling is required when using turmeric, as anything it comes into contact with may be stained a fetching shade of bright yellow.

INDEX

COOKBOOKS BY THE CROSSING PRESS

Homestyle Cooking Series

Homestyle Chinese Cooking
By Yan-kit So

These delicious recipes include the six primary ways in which the Wok may be used, from Soups, Steaming, and Stir-frying, to Sautéing, Deep-frying, and Braising. Anyone, from beginners to accomplished cooks, will find this book useful.

$16.95 • Paper • ISBN 0-89594-883-4

Homestyle Italian Cooking
By Lori Carangelo

These wonderful dishes use fresh ingredients, carefully prepared to bring out the special flavors of the best, homestyle Italian cooking.

$16.95 • Paper • ISBN 0-89594-867-2

Homestyle Mexican Cooking
By Lourdes Nichols

This tantalizing collection of over 180 authentic recipes from Mexican cuisine includes meat and poultry dishes and recipes for rice dishes, vegetables, salads, desserts, and drinks.

$16.95 • Paper • ISBN 0-89594-861-3

Homestyle Middle Eastern Cooking
By Pat Chapman

This collection of authentic recipes features spicy regional dishes selected from hundreds of recipes the author collected on his travels throughout the Middle East.

$16.95 • Paper • ISBN 0-89594-860-5

Homestyle Thai and Indonesian Cooking
By Sri Owen

Sri Owen offers authentic recipes for satés, curries, fragrant rice dishes, spicy vegetables, and snacks and sweets. Includes adaptations using Western ingredients.

$16.95 • Paper • ISBN 0-89594-859-1

COOKBOOKS BY THE CROSSING PRESS

Specialty Series

Biscotti, Bars, and Brownies
by Terri Henry

This collection of easy-to-follow recipes presents more than 70 recipes for cookies baked in a pan.

$6.95 • Paper • ISBN 0-89594-901-6

Old World Breads
by Charel Scheele

Discover the art of old world bread-making. Instructions are given to get brick oven results from an ordinary oven using a simple clay flower-pot saucer.

$6.95 • Paper • ISBN 0-89594-902-4

Quick Breads
by Howard Early and Glenda Morris

Quick breads mix up in ten to fifteen minutes and go straight from the mixing bowl to the oven. Enjoy white, rye, wheat, scones, muffins—the range of quick breads is limited only by the imagination.

$6.95 • Paper • ISBN 0-89594-941-5

Salad Dressings
by Teresa H. Burns

Making fresh salad dressing is easy! This little book is full of creative dressings that are fresh, healthy, and delicious.

$6.95 • Paper • ISBN 0-89594-895-8

Sun-Dried Tomatoes
by Andrea Chesman

Chesman's simple recipes include a selection of appetizers, salads, pastas, and breads as well as instructions for drying tomatoes at home.

$6.95 • Paper • ISBN 0-89594-900-8

Wholesome Cookies
by Jane Marsh Dieckman

Nothing has been left out of these melt-in-your-mouth confections, but plenty has been added—in the form of nonfat dry milk, fruits, nuts, seeds, bran, and wheat germ to boost the nutritional value of each cookie, while providing plenty of good taste, crunch,and natural sweetness

$6.95 • Paper • ISBN 0-89594-942-3

Cookbooks by The Crossing Press

From Bengal to Punjab
The Cuisines of India
By Smita Chandra

Homestyle Indian food featuring recipes and techniques handed down through generations of the author's family; breads, barbeque fare, spice blends and chutneys.

$12.95 • Paper • ISBN 0-89594-509-6

The Spice Box
Vegetarian Indian Cookbook
By Manju Shivraj Singh

"An imaginative collection of recipes that will be of interest to the seasoned chef of Indian cuisine. A cookbook well suited to the adventurous vegetarian." —*Publishers Weekly*

$12.95 • Paper • ISBN 0-89594-053-1

Taste of the Tropics
Traditional and Innovative Cooking from the Pacific and Caribbean
By Jay Solomon

Part travelogue, part cookbook, with helpful hints and tasty tips for using tropical ingredients, this book is the next best thing to being there!

$10.95 • Paper • ISBN 0-89594-533-9

Traveling Jamaica with Knife, Fork & Spoon
By Robb Walsh and Jay McCarthy

Take an adventurous trip across the island of Jamaica with 140 recipes and dozens of colorful characters along the way.

$16.95 • Paper • ISBN 0-89594-698-X

To receive a current catalog from The Crossing Press
please call toll-free, 800-777-1048.
Visit our Web site on the Internet: www.crossingpress.com